Constitutional Economics

IEA Masters of Modern Economics

Series editor: Cento Veljanovski

James M. Buchanan	*Constitutional Economics*
Milton Friedman	*Monetarist Economics*
Friedrich A. Hayek	*Economic Freedom*

Constitutional Economics

James M. Buchanan

Basil Blackwell

First published 1991

Basil Blackwell Ltd
108 Cowley Road, Oxford OX4 1JF, UK

Basil Blackwell, Inc.
3 Cambridge Center
Cambridge, Massachusetts 02142, USA

British Library Cataloguing in Publication Data

A CIP catalogue record for this book is available from the British Library.

Library of Congress Cataloging in Publication Data

Buchanan, James M.
Constitutional economics / James M. Buchanan.
p.   cm. — (IEA masters of modern economics)
Includes bibliographical references.
ISBN 0–631–17108–8
1. Social choice. 2. Economic policy. I. Title. II. Series.
HB846.8.B78   1990
338.9—dc20   89–78250   CIP

Typeset in $10\frac{1}{2}$ on 12 pt Sabon
by Butler & Tanner Ltd, Frome and London
Printed in Great Britain by Butler & Tanner Ltd, Frome and London

Contents

Introduction

The economics of 'public' – as distinct from private – choice in the last 30 years, the new political economy, has subjected the activities of government to the systematic micro-economic analysis of the political behaviour of its individuals and institutions long applied to the commercial behaviour of individuals and institutions in the market.

It has produced a more penetrating and realistic understanding of democratic representative government than presented by conventional political science, especially in Britain, which largely bypassed its economics: its costs as well as benefits, its government 'failure' to contrast with market 'failure', its dispensable as well as unavoidable collective functions (the so-called 'public goods'). Public choice has produced an economics of government to place alongside the economics of the market.

Since economic activity in government as well as the market confronts the same conflict between potentially unlimited demand and severely limited supply, but in a more severe form since government dispenses widely with price and has to evolve other methods of rationing, it may seem a surprising neglect of the economists until recent decades to have failed to dissect 'public' choice in the representative institutions of government as closely and critically as they dissected private choice by individuals in the market.

The philosophers and economists of the classical tradition sensed the shortcomings of politics and often evinced little respect for politicians. David Hume's admonition was unequivocal: 'in contriving any system of government ... every man ought to be supposed a knave, and to have no other end ... than private interest'.[1] Adam Smith's more familiar dismissal of politicians spurned them as 'crafty and insidious animals'.[2] John Stuart Mill echoed Hume: 'the very principle of constitutional government requires it to be assumed, that political power will be abused to promote the particular purposes of the holder'.[3] And Alfred Marshall's contrast between imagined and real government was crystal-clear: 'Do you mean government all wise, all just, all powerful or government as it is now?'[4]

Even with the modern experience of the inadequacies, errors, myopia, and corruptions of government, it may be difficult for the citizen to accept that men and women freely elected or appointed into 'public' office nevertheless serve their own purposes. It seems to be a reflection on the judgement of the elector that he has elected into 'public' office people no better than himself. The instinctive hope is that they are in a class apart from other, undistinguished, men and women engaged in the daily round of earning a living. The reality would be accepted more readily if it were seen as a conflict of interest: the elected cannot be expected to put their interests below and subordinate to those of the electors; they must be expected to use power and influence for their advantage. The electors may benefit, but characteristically from activities designed to benefit the elected. Except in national emergency, when all humans become heroes, the rest is vanity.

Beyond the instinctive classical realism on political people there were seminal antecedents of public-choice analysis in the public finance and other writings of 19th- and 20th-century Swedish and Italian economists, recalled in Professor Sir Alan Peacock's 1989 Mattioli Lectures, *Public Choice Analysis in Historical Perspective*. And they have infused the work of contemporary public choice economists. British public choice has developed on parallel but not identical lines. As a leading British public choice scholar, Scottish by absorption, Professor Peacock's further thinking in British public choice is reviewed in a volume of essays, *Public Choice, Public Finance and Public Policy*, by former colleagues and students. Yet the essentials are common to the USA and Britain, as well as to countries in Europe and other continents. Professor John Williamson related the lag before he turned from 'the comforting Fabian assumption ... that governments were essentially benevolent social institutions' to the Peacock Critique that 'governments are run by politicians and bureaucrats who may be maximising a party or individual welfare function [schedule of preferences] rather than any half-respectable specification of a social welfare function [a schedule that assimilates all individual preferences into a supposed general social preference]'.

Yet in conventional political science people in 'public' life still appear to be a race apart: politicians, bureaucrats, and their acolytes called to serve the public interest with scant self-regard for their own. In contrast to the classical scepticism, conventional political science, predominantly collectivist in sentiment, created an uncritical appraisal of the competence and potential of political people to serve the public interest that propelled the massive expansion in government of the past century.

Yet both the censorious classics and the sanguine collectivists were judgemental: the new public choice economists and other scholars are analytical. They are not disappointed: they analyse people in politics as other men and women in other human activities – neither saints nor sinners but fallible humans confronted by the necessity to make the most of scarce resources, and understandably conscious of the interests about them more than of those more distant that they are not as competent to judge.

The principles and the approach of modern public choice are generally regarded as having been systematised in the seminal work of the Americans (of Scottish ancestry), Professors J. M. Buchanan and Gordon Tullock in 1962, *The Calculus of Consent*, where Buchanan analysed politics as a process of 'exchange' between governmental rent-yielding and group interest rent-seeking (under the influence of the Swedish Wicksell's work in public finance) and Tullock (with his experience of bureaucracy in government) analysed the motivations of 'public choosers', voters, and politicians as well as bureaucrats.

Elements of modern public choice were foreshadowed by the American Anthony Downs on motives in voting and by the Scottish Duncan Black on the decisions of representative committees, and further back by the doubts about the ability of electoral processes to reflect voters' intentions elucidated by the 19th-century Oxford mathematician Charles Dodgson, also known as Lewis Carroll, and the 18th-century Frenchmen Condorcet, Borda, and Leplace.

The Buchanan–Tullock book spawned a new development of economic reasoning and research in the activities of government, democracy, bureaucracy, politics, and many offshoots mainly in the USA but also in Britain and in Switzerland and other European countries. In the USA the intellectual ferment at the Center for the Study of Public Choice, originally in Charlottesville, then at Blacksburg, now at George Mason University, has spread to other universities. The main British academics are Professors Peacock (Heriot–Watt University), Jack Wiseman (York), Charles K. Rowley (George Mason), and Martin Ricketts (Buckingham); and in Switzerland Professors Peter Bernholz and Bruno Frey, in Italy Francisco Forte, in Canada Albert Breton, and others in Norway, Spain, and elsewhere.

Men and women elected as politicians or appointed as 'public' officials are not transformed into public benefactors. They have access to vastly more resources but, compared with people in the market, they are more likely to use them ill rather than well since they largely lack the guidance of pricing, they can avoid retribution for their harmful decisions, they are using other people's money, and they are inherently unaccountable for their errors because the costs of their decisions are usually distant and incalculable.

Public choice is concerned with the micro-economic market question of how much citizen–consumers value government services sufficiently to pay for them, rather than with the macro-economic political decision of how many citizen–voters value them enough to vote for a party or a politician.

The study of public choice, belatedly recognised after 30 years in the award of the Nobel Prize to Professor James Buchanan, was originally described as 'non-market decision-making', an inelegant but precise description of the proceedings of representatives in collectives, from committees to parliaments, making decisions for constituents. 'Public choice' is simpler but unfortunate since, unlike the market where choices are made directly 'by' the public, the collective process makes choices indirectly 'for' the public. And that is the source of the conflict between what the public would have chosen and what its representatives predominantly choose for it.

Government is no longer to be seen as the impartial referee who sets the by-laws by which the economic 'game' in the market is played, but a powerful participant in the game, much more powerful than the individuals or firms and other 'players', and liable to ignore or bend the by-laws to its advantage, always claiming that it did so in the general interest of the other players. The notion of government as the impartial chairman or referee is a myth of convential political science that has proliferated the *étatism* that infected all British political parties.

The study of public choice is in effect the economics of politics. And in 30 short years it has revealed why representative government, of which Abraham Lincoln held high hopes on the battlefield of Gettysburg during the American civil war, had given 'democracy' a bad name. The weaknesses of conventional political science are compounded by the journalists in the American and British press who enthuse about the return of 'democracy' to the socialist countries without analysing its imperfection: its chronic susceptibility to 'government failure'. We have yet to devise means to remove its imperfections, its obstacles to Lincoln's vision; by electoral machinery that will make it government 'of' the people, by constitutional or other controls over its mechanisms and new machinery such as electronic voting (although relevant only for public goods) that will make it government 'by' the people, and disciplines on its rent-giving to make it government 'for' the people.

Professor Buchanan put the essence of his teaching into three lines in a recent essay: 'It is critically important that we recapture the 18th century wisdom ... [on] checks and balance to limit government ... and shed once and for all the romantically idiotic notion that as long as [political] processes are democratic all is fair game.'[5] Professor Buchanan's strictures on superficial thinking apply no less in Britain and Europe.

The title of this collection of Professor Buchanan's six IEA contributions from 1965 to 1989, *Constitutional Economics*, is also the name given by American public choice economists to their development and refinement of the economics of politics. (The American emphasis is also shown in the title of a 1984 collection of papers edited by Richard Mackenzie on 'Containing the Economic Powers of Government'.)[6] The IEA texts indicate some of the main elements in Professor Buchanan's thinking over much of the 30 years.

The 'key-note' *Paper* was the opening address to a seminar assembled in 1978 when it was considered that, in spite of almost 20 years of exposition, the essence of public choice had made little impact on British academic, political, or public thinking. Further papers were contributed by Professors Albert Breton of Canada, Frey, Peacock, Rowley, and Wiseman. The intention was to reinforce the earlier *Paper* in 1976 by the other founding father of public choice, Professor Tullock, to explain the essentials in *The Vote Motive*.

Professor Buchanan compressed into 5,500 words the historical evaluation of the new economics of politics and indicated the fundamental issues it was raising that were left unexplained by conventional political science: whether majority voting can elect 'representative government' that faithfully represents the public interest, whether government can provide the 'public goods' (perform the unavoidably collective functions) on which individuals differ, whether politicians can be expected to act as benevolent despots, whether public officials can be expected to act as economic eunuchs, whether rent-seeking can be resisted, and whether government that fails these and other tests can be disciplined and controlled by constitutions.

These implied strictures on conventional political science had been foreshadowed in a short *Paper* on *The Inconsistencies of the National Health Service* during a brief visit to Britain in 1965. The then early failures of the NHS, evident in the professional dissatisfaction, threatened resignations, reduced recruiting, replacement of home-trained by immigrant hospital staffs, overcrowding, delays in treatment, and more could be rectified not by the appointment of wiser men (still the recourse of government) but by no less than structural reform in the financing mechanism. The political cancer in the NHS was the conflict between the collective, politicised, supply of medical care in response to individual demand. It had divorced supply from demand: individuals as consumers would demand more 'free' (unpriced) medical care than they were prepared to supply and pay for as taxpaying voters.

If it was true in 1965 it is still true in 1990. But government has not learned to remove the structural conflict diagnosed by Professor Buchanan. A successful business administrator has been appointed to administer the NHS, but without the pricing that had enabled him to make a success of his business. And, despite innovations such as internal markets, family doctor budgets, and opting out by hospitals, the NHS remains a politicised artefact: supply is still controlled by the political process and its financing of 'free' services by taxation extracted from reluctant voters. The gap left by markets in public services has been filled inadequately by opinion polls based on economic theory that would fail first-year economics undergraduates, that price has no effect on demand, and that elicit the hardly significant hypothetical information that individual taxpayers want more welfare services paid for by other taxpayers. The British, in short, 25 years after Professor Buchanan wrote in 1965, are in practice still refusing to finance as taxpayers and voters the unlimited medical care they are demanding at nil prices as patients. The NHS has induced the British to tolerate less or worse medical care than they could pay for, and would pay for if they were able to pay in ways they preferred.

Two *Hobart Papers* with co-authors, *The Consequences of Mr Keynes* in 1978 and *Monopoly in Money and Inflation* in 1981, enabled Professor Buchanan to apply public choice analysis to the great issues of the day. The most damaging 'consequence' of Mr Keynes was not only in economics but also in politics. His cure of budget deficits for underemployment in a market economy was not only economically defective, as the monetary economists led by Professor Milton Friedman had shown; possibly even worse, it was politically unrealistic. It was based on the 'romantic' notion, inherited from conventional political scientists, that politicians would alternate politically popular budget deficits with politically unpopular budget surpluses.

In *The Consequences of Mr Keynes* the argument was that the instrument Keynes had fashioned could not be used in a representative democracy: Keynes had 'turned the politicians loose' to overspend, overborrow, over-print money, and over-inflate. And in many countries they had run amok. It has taken a government sufficiently imbued with the teachings of public choice to see the irrelevance of the price-less opinion polls, and to anticipate that well-timed tax-reductions are likely to be more agreeable to the voters than tax-increases to pay for even more wasteful 'welfare' services, to resist the importunities of its Departments and bureaucrats for still higher expenditure on the welfare state.

Monopoly in Money and Inflation in 1981 was a further assault on the state monopoly for reasons of the political temptation to secure revenue by inflation, rather than by economic efficiency, such as the argument of Professor Frederick Hayek that only competing private suppliers of currencies would maintain their value, since uncontrolled increases in supply would destroy their value and precipitate inflation. The conclusion, that the solution lay in reform of the monetary régime by a new monetary constitution, was also different from that of the monetarists, who proposed reform in monetary policy. The recent proposal of the British Chancellor of the Exchequer for competing national currencies in place of the unified EEC currency is a compromise between a government monopoly and competing *private* currencies: public choice analysis suggests doubts whether national governments would play the game by the new rules rather than conspire to politicise the system by agreements on exchange rates.

Professor Buchanan's solution for both unrestrained budgetary deficits and the state monopoly of money was to discipline democracy: to erect monetary and budgetary rules and institutions that disciplined government, put into writing and made part of the constitution, to be changed only by substantial majorities of the people (but in direct referenda voting rather than in representative assemblies).

In 1986 a contribution to *The Unfinished Agenda* led Professor Buchanan to emphasise a development in modern economies that made constitutional reform urgent. The modern state had become the vehicle for 'massive transfers of wealth'. Their extended powers induced politicians to compete for votes by offering short-term social benefits, to the neglect of the adverse long-term consequences on the populace. The career politician not interested in long-term socio-political viability had largely replaced the former statesman-politician who could take a long view.

Here, at least, public choice was diagnosing a dilemma in representative democracy that only a change in the rules governing the powers of short-term politicians could treat. This dilemma in the political process, that representatives elected to take a wider and longer view than the citizens who elected them were ironically governed by political myopia, the 'short-termism' alleged against the market, raised complex questions in the design of political institutions: the optimum period of legislatures, the power to legislate for future citizens who have no vote in the present, the enactment of 'irreversible' policies, the pre-election timing of expansionary economic impulses for party-political advantage, the very range of functions permitted to government, not least the nature of 'public goods', the obligation to repeal measures outdated by events, and more.

If democracy permits or incites temporary majorities to legislate for immediate effect, irresponsibly indifferent to the long-term consequences, it is at the mercy of the cynical politics of *après nous la déluge*. The political process then incites even good men to do lasting harm. Attlee left a deluge of bureaucratic welfare, Macmillan and Wilson a deluge of corporatism, Heath a deluge of inflation, most post-war Conservative and Labour Prime Ministers a deluge of unnecessary monopoly, superfluous bureaucracy and excessive taxes. The new political democracy in the communist countries does not solve the dilemmas of democracy. The hope was that government would resolve 'market failure'; it has emerged with the even more intractable 'failure' of representative democracy. Government is self-inflationary; it is not the dependable cure of known diseases but the unrestrained cause of new diseases.

A further contribution in 1981 was an essay with Professor Tullock in *The Emerging Consensus*, a collection to celebrate the 25th year of the IEA. It proposed a 'leap forward' from the study of markets to constitutional change. The advance was to be to 'the incentives, the rewards, and the penalties' of the politicians and their bureaucrats and the new institutions in which these inducements were more calculated to induce them to work to the general advantage. Conventional orthodox political science offered little solution. It was to be sought rather in recapturing the wisdom of the 18th century: its 'scepticism about the abilities of politics, of government, to handle detailed regulatory tasks, to go beyond the limits of the "minimal" or "protection" state'.

The Buchanan–Tullock espousal of the 'minimal' state opens for liberals the central question of the functions of government. In his eloquent *Hobart Paper* 113, Dr John Gray argued persuasively for the wider functions of the 'limited' state. The whole ground has recently been traversed by Professor Joseph Stiglitz in *The Economic Rôle of the State*, which favours the wider limited than the narrower minimal rôle. And Professor Israel Kirzner in his latest work, *Discovery, Capitalism and Distributive Justice*, envisages a reduced rôle for government by the argument, which circumvents John Rawls's on a larger rôle and Robert Nozick's on a smaller, that, since new resources and products are not taken from others but are newly discovered and created by individuals, 'social justice' does not require the wide redistributive functions by government envisaged in conventional political science.

Professor Buchanan's latest IEA contribution to date was to apply public choice to the market-oriented reforms of the USA in the 1980s in *Reagonomics and After* and its implications for the rôle and structure of government, some of which may apply to the Thatcher Governments so far. He judged the Reagan presidency as 'a failed opportunity to secure the structural changes that might have been within the realms of the politically possible'.

These judgements on the Reagan 'lost opportunity' raise the most fundamental issue in the over-expansion of government in representative democracy and its containment by constitutional discipline. For Britain, as well as for the USA, the questions suggested by public choice analysis are: Can government be expected to preside over its own dissolution? Can the excesses of the political process – not least the influence of rent-seeking pressure groups – be removed by action within the political process?

The pressure groups, like the regulated who capture the regulators, must be expected to manipulate political opinion on the new constitutional constraints. The bureaucrats are adept at drafting new measures to allow them discretionary powers that frustrate the purpose of the restraints. The lawyers and solicitors must be expected to interpret the amendments in their interests. (In Britain they have not taken kindly to measures that limited their restrictive practices.) In short, the self-disciplining of over-government will itself be a highly politicised process in which political people – the politicians in power and the bureaucrats who serve them – will be judge and jury.

The solution, especially in Britain with an unwritten constitution, may have to be the creation of an overwhelming public philosophy in favour of less government. It must come to be believed that government is a wayward servant inclined to self-aggrandisement, a glutton for power, and given to hypocrisy in concealing empire-building by protestations of saintly intentions. The Fabians began in the 1880s to create in all parties a sentiment in favour of more government that eased the path of socialisation in the last century. The antidote may have to be to create an equal but opposite sentiment in favour of less government that will ease de-socialisation in the coming decades. This is the task the IEA set itself in 1957; and it has been powerfully reinforced by the teachings of public choice developed by Professor Buchanan in the USA and by the growing army of libertarian economists, political scientists, historians, lawyers, and philosophers in Britain and Europe.

Arthur Seldon

Notes

1   David Hume, 'Of the Independancy of Parliament' (1741) in *Essays Moral, Political and Literary*, Liberty Classics, 1985, p. 42.
2   Adam Smith, *The Wealth of Nations*, 1776.
3   J. S. Mill, *Considerations on Representative Government* (1861), in *Essays in Politics and Society*, University of Toronto Press, 1977, p. 505.
4   Alfred Marshall, in A. E. Benians (ed.), *Memorials of Alfred Marshall*, Macmillan, 1926.
5   J. M. Buchanan, 'Constitutional Imperatives for the 1990s: the Legal Order for a Free and Productive Economy', in *Thinking About America*, Hoover Institution, 1988.
6   Richard Mackenzie (ed.), *Constitutional Economics*, D. C. Heath, Lexington, Mass., 1984. This American emphasis is also shown in a 1989 collection, *Public Choice and Constitutional Economics*, edited by J. D. Gwartney and R. E. Wagner, Greenwich, Conn.: JAI Press.

1

Post-Reagan Political Economy

1 Introduction

I propose to discuss the post-Reagan political economy of the United States, a subject that surely has some relevance for the political economy of the United Kingdom. It is possible to make some relatively secure predictions about the sort of problems that will arise. The Reagan record has been written, and we can define the 'roads not taken' during eight years with some accuracy. Any discussion of the post-Reagan political economy will necessarily involve an assessment of the Reagan presidency, one that is specifically limited here to the political economy of policy.

My theme is both simple and familiar. I assess the Reagan presidency as one of failed opportunity to secure the structural changes that might have been within the realms of the politically possible. The result is that, after Reagan, the institutions in place will remain roughly the same as those existing in 1980. And the potential for mutual and reciprocal exploitation through the political process, the behavioural domain of those persons and groups (the rent-seekers) that seek private gain through the agencies of government, will not have been substantially reduced in range and scope.

On the other hand, the shift in public attitudes that made the Reagan ascendancy possible will not be reversed by a shift in administration. There will be no return to the romantic delusion that the national government offers cures for all problems: real, imagined, evolved, or invented. After Reagan we shall live in a political economy that embodies widespread public scepticism about government's capacities, and also

Published originally as a contribution to IEA Readings No. 28, *Reaganomics and After* (1989).

about the purity of the motivations of political agents. But, as noted, at the same time we shall have in place all of the institutional trappings that emerged during the apogee of our romantic interlude with politicisation.

The struggle between interest groups

Politics involves playing many simultaneous games with and between shifting coalitions of interests. Broadly, however, it is useful to think of politics, post-Reagan, as a struggle between the rent-seekers, who try to secure private profits or rents through the authority of government, and the constitutionalists, who seek to constrain this authority. And it is important to recognise that all of us, or almost all, are likely to play on both sides of this super game simultaneously. We behave as rent-seekers when we support expanded spending programmes or tax breaks to benefit our own industry, occupation, region, local authority, or, quite simply, our own pet version of some 'public interest'. We shall behave as constitutionalists when we recognise the overreaching of government in general.

This struggle will proceed independently of the particular electoral results of 1988. The apparent competition among and between personalities and parties will matter much less than the struggle within each of us, as citizens, between resort to politics and explicit search for limits on politics. The question is clear: Without the putative legitimacy that was provided by the romantic delusion, can the rent-seekers dominate the constitutionalists? Or will the return to some semblance of the 18th-century wisdom about the potential for abuse of political authority generate, in turn, some effective embodiment of the 18th-century limits on this authority?

A modern constitutionalism?

In one sense, we may read the Reagan era in the United States as an interlude between the romantic follies represented by Kennedy's Camelot and Johnson's Great Society, and one of the two post-Reagan options that I have suggested. The first post-Reagan scenario involves the raw struggle of interests in majoritarian politics constrained by no constitutional limits; the second post-Reagan scenario could reflect the beginnings of a return to some modern version of the dream of James Madison. And we should make no mistake that one of these two outcomes (or a mixture of the two) must describe post-Reagan political economy. The basic struggle was exemplified in the arguments of the 1988 presidential aspirants, both of whom seemed unwilling to challenge the rent-seekers directly while at the same time both seemed to recognise that rent-seeking demands must be constrained.

In Section 2, I explain my verdict that the Reagan leadership is one of lost opportunity. In Section 3, I shall briefly examine the Reagan fiscal policy agenda, and relate this agenda to more comprehensive issues. In Section 4, I describe the change in perception and consequent evaluation of politics and politicians that has occurred only since the 1960s. In Section 5, I discuss the supergame between the rent-seekers and the constitutionalists in more detail. And finally, in Section 6, I relate the argument to American constitutional democracy, by comparison and contrast with the parliamentary democracy of the United Kingdom.

2 Policy Within Politics versus Structural Reform

Those who are familiar with my various writings will recognise that it is necessary here to review briefly the methodological perspective of the constitutional economist. Some appreciation of this perspective is required in order to understand my assessment of the Reagan enterprise. There is a categorical distinction to be made between playing the policy game within the rules of ordinary politics and engaging in the wider exercise of considering the rules themselves, by which I mean the institutional–constitutional structure that constrains the workings of politics.

A central objective of the Reagan presidency was to reduce the politicisation of the national economy, to reverse in direction a movement that had been going on for almost a century. In political economy terms, the characteristic feature of this century has been the growth in size and scope of the public sector, along with the increasing concentration of authority in the central or federal government. This feature has not, of course, been unique to the United States. The 20th century has been characterised by the growth of government everywhere.

Fixed rules or incentive structures

There are two ways in which the Reagan objective of reduced politicisation might have been approached. The first, which I have called 'policy within politics', embodies the presumption that the rules, the institutional–constitutional structure from which political decisions emerge, are fixed. By inference, the failure of pre-Reagan politics to have advanced the cause of depoliticisation was attributed to the presence of the 'wrong' parties and the 'wrong' politicians in positions of decision-making authority. In this view, the specific task for the dominant coalition of Reagan supporters was to repeal and reverse policy steps taken by the pre-Reagan 'socialists' of all stripes.

The constitutional economist, who might have shared the stipulated objective of depoliticisation, would not have accepted this interpretation of the Reagan enterprise. His was a totally different diagnosis of the pre-Reagan political economy. The increasing politicisation of the national economy over this century was attributed, not to the preferences of ideologically driven political coalitions, but to the incentive structure embedded in the existing institutions from which political choices emerge. In this approach, it matters relatively little, if at all, which parties or which politicians succeed or fail in the overt electoral competition. The constitutional economist would have based his expectations for any permanent change only in modifications of the incentive structure.

As might have been anticipated, there were elements of both of these approaches in the early Reagan rhetoric. There was talk of the need to change the rules, as well as of great things to be expected when the 'other side' was thrown out and 'our men' put in their place. In 1980 and earlier, Ronald Reagan supported the proposal for a constitutional amendment to require the federal government to balance its budget and to impose limits on rates of growth in total spending. He also promised, in his campaign rhetoric of 1980, to eliminate the cabinet-level departments of education and energy.

It was evident, however, even before inauguration in January 1981, that the Reagan leadership was to move primarily if not exclusively along the policy-within-politics route and to relegate to secondary status any attempt to achieve genuine structural change. Early proposals to examine the structure of arrangements for monetary authority were rejected; the balanced-budget amendment was not supported during the early months; no mention was made of the promised elimination of departments. These were opportunities that were lost by the new administration from the time it took office. The Reagan administration became itself a part of the existing structure; it could no longer succeed in generating changes in the structure itself. All it was left with was to play the standard political game.

3 Taxing, Spending, and Debt

The stipulated objective of reducing the politicisation of the national economy was widely shared by the American electorate in the 1980s. One measure of the extent of politicisation is the size and rate of increase in the federal government's budget, the total rate of expenditure. There was general support for President Reagan's argument that programme spending was, in general, grossly over-extended and that rates of tax were too high, and had been allowed to increase too rapidly during the inflation of the 1970s.

A meaningful criterion for policy designed to reduce the rate of increase in federal outlay is the present value of anticipated outlay over an indefinite period. A policy designed to reduce rates of increase in current-period outlay only at the cost of ensuring increased rates of spending in later periods would not seem defensible. Yet this short-term policy is precisely the one followed by the Reagan administration. Projected rates of increase in tax revenues were cut in 1981, but *without* correspondingly reduced rates of increase in federal spending. The increased shortfall of revenues behind the increase in outlay was residually financed by the sale of debt, that is, by incurring budget deficits.

The result was that, for the Reagan years, taxpayers had available, for private disposition, an expanded level of purchasing power, relative to that which would have been available under a scenario that matched cuts in rates of increase in taxes and in government spending. This result seems appropriate only if the objective was to give more funds to individuals during the Reagan years, in disregard of the effects in subsequent years. What will be these latter effects, given the policy history sketched out? The outlays during the Reagan years, and before, that were financed by debt must be 'paid for' during the post-Reagan years by service charges represented in interest payments. To the extent that interest charges become a necessary component in the federal budget, these charges will be matched dollar-for-dollar by reductions in funds available for private disposition. The increase in the funds available for private disposition during the Reagan years is precisely matched by the reduction in funds available for private disposition during post-Reagan years. The deficit financing of Reagan-year spending will have accomplished nothing other than a displacement of real cost in time, which is what the classical theory of public debt emphasised.

The effect of the budget deficit

Can the Reagan fiscal policy be defended in terms of the present-value criterion suggested above? Did the residual financing of outlay by debt, with mounting deficits, exert pressures on the Congress to hold down rates of increase in spending more than would have been exerted through tax financing? This argument was, indeed, prominent in the Reagan White House. By forcing a political disequilibrium between the two financing sources, taxes and debt, through the initial 1981 marginal-rate reduction of tax, the politically supportable rates of spending might have been lower than that rate financed by an equilibrium adjustment between the two financing sources. This argument would, however, seem to fly in the face of more elementary public-choice logic which suggests that political decision-makers, like individuals in their private capacities, will tend to spend more when the borrowing option is present than when it is not. The precise weights to be given to these offsetting arguments cannot be assigned here.

Nevertheless, the legacy of the Reagan fiscal policy is not in dispute. In post-Reagan years, the funds available for private disposition by individuals must be lower than if tax increases had kept pace with increases in expenditure. The costs of spending during the Reagan years will be borne by taxpayers and/or frustrated programme beneficiaries (and holders of government debt instruments if indirect or direct default is considered an option). Rates of tax will be higher and/or rates of spending on public programmes will be lower than they would have been under the alternative financing régime. The commonly observed comment about chickens coming home to roost is appropriate.

How might this result have been avoided if a structural approach to policy had been followed? It seems clear that Reagan's early mandate was sufficient to have secured approval of a constitutional amendment to require budget balance and to impose limits on rates of increase in federal spending. This policy package, with an appropriate phase-in period before balance in the budget was to be achieved, would not have reduced rates of increase in taxes so dramatically as experienced under the Reagan presidency. Rates of outlay might have increased less than those we have observed during these years, although, as I suggested above, this conclusion may be debated by economists using different models. But the important conclusion which cannot be rejected is that, in post-Reagan years, citizens, whether as taxpayers, programme beneficiaries, or creditors, will be worse off than they would have been under the suggested alternative for policy.

4 Politics and Politicians Post-Reagan

The fiscal legacy alone places major constraints on the flexibility of response of any political coalition in the post-Reagan years. It will prove difficult to mount support for new programmes of spending, given the size of the budget deficit and the large interest component included in it. The threat or existence of emerging deficits may or may not have constrained rates of spending, relative to those rates that would have been supported under tax financing, in the 1980s. The existence of the accumulated debt, with its accompanying interest charges, must constrain rates of spending in the 1990s. This fiscal constraint may, however, be somewhat unimportant relative to the more principled constraint embodied in the attitude of the citizenry towards politics and politicians.

We can, I think, be assured that there will be no return, post-Reagan, to the romantic illusion that characterised politics during the 1960s. The Reagan presidency represented an anti-politics mentality on the part of the citizenry (the electorate), a mentality that reflected a fundamental shift in public attitudes over the decades of the 1970s and 1980s. It may be useful here to review this dramatic shift in public opinion.

The growth of government

I noted earlier that the first two-thirds of this century were characterised by a dramatic growth in the size of the public or governmental sector of the economy, whether this growth be measured by rates of increase in public spending, taxation, regulation or some other broader standard. Such growth rates were not, or course, unique to the USA. Indeed, the UK and other nations of Western Europe experienced even more dramatic increases than the US over the same period. In the USA this politicisation of economic life occurred in several distinct stages. A potted history may be useful.

The 'progressive era' that describes the turn of the century embodied attitudes that were highly critical of the unbridled market economy and offered the arguments for later politicised interferences. The 1913 enactment of the 16th amendment to the US written constitution authorised the levying of a progressive income tax. This amendment was critically important because income tax provided a source of revenue that would grow disproportionately with the growth in national income, either real or nominal. World War I, as all other wars, expanded the central government's authority, and, although there was considerable depoliticisation in the 1920s, the instruments of authority remained in place. Franklin Roosevelt's New Deal, as a response to the economic emergency of the Great Depression, reflected widespread public support for new, expanded, and often ill-conceived, programmes of governmental activity. World War II followed and, once again, the crisis itself facilitated an increase in government's authority.[1]

Eisenhower's 1950s were characterised by much less political retrenchment than the 1920s. The decade of the 1950s in the United States is best described as a holding operation. There followed the bizarre decade of the 1960s, which witnessed the apogee of public support for politicisation at least a decade later than the comparable situation in the UK. The artificial and essentially romantic ideas of Kennedy's Camelot were, however, well on the way to exposure and prospective oblivion when the 1963 assassination of Kennedy and the subsequent ascendancy of Lyndon Johnson provided the impetus required to enact left-over New Deal legislation that was three decades out of date.

The romantic delusion

In retrospect, from our vantage point in 1988, it seems amazing that this whole period of dramatic growth in the politicisation of economic life in the USA and elsewhere, occurred in the absence of any plausibly realistic theory of how politics actually works. We were everywhere trapped in the romantic delusion stemming from Hegelian idealism: the state was, somehow, a benevolent entity and those who made decisions on behalf of the state were guided by consideration of the general or public interest. Thus welfare economists considered there was a *prima facie* case for politicisation of an activity once the market was judged to have failed to meet the idealised criterion of maximal efficiency.

The set of attitudes which embodies these ideas was shifted in the 1960s and beyond. There are two identifiable reasons for the change.

First of all, in the USA, Lyndon Johnson's extensions of the welfare state failed demonstrably in many instances; these failures were directly observed by citizens as well as by research scholars and specialists. The failures were often described in terms of the 'capture' of programmes by special-interest beneficiaries whose motivation seemed to be private and personal gains.

The second identifiable reason for the shift in attitude towards politicisation was the development and promulgation of a theory of how politics actually works, along with accompanying analyses of how politicians actually behave. Public choice theory, broadly defined, came along in the 1960s, 1970s, and 1980s to offer intellectual foundations that allowed citizens to understand the political failures they were able to observe at first hand. This theory, in its simplest terms, does little more than to extend the behavioural model used by economists to choices made by persons in political rôles (as voters, politicians, bureaucrats). Once this elementary shift in vision is made, however, the critical flaw in the idealised model of politics and politicians is exposed. No longer could the romanticised model of the workings of the state be tolerated.

Identifying special interests

Politics was, for the first time in two centuries, seen as a very complex interaction process, in which many persons, in many rôles, seek a whole set of divergent objectives, which include a large measure of their own private economic gains. Politicians in elected office seek re-election, and this dictates that they be responsive to the desires of constituents. And constituents seek to profit from politics just as they seek to profit from their private activities. Politics, as a game among competing special-interest groups, each of which is organised for the pursuit of profit through the arms and agencies of the state, takes on a wholly different colouration in the post-1960s from that which it assumed in the decades before the 1960s.

The reaction on the part of the public was that which might have been anticipated. By the mid-1970s, the rhetoric of anti-politics had entered the political debates. Both the 1976 Carter and, more emphatically, the 1980 Reagan electoral successes stemmed from this shift in public attitudes, as did the 1979 Thatcher victory in the UK. For more than a decade the electorates have viewed politics and politicians more realistically than they have done for more than a century.

I have traced out this history because it is helpful in making projections of the post-Reagan political economy. I should emphasise that there will be no return to the romantic delusion about politics that characterised public and academic attitudes throughout most of this century. The socialist god is emotionally and intellectually dead. Despite the occasional rhetorical flourish from the old left and its political spokesmen, no political leader, post-Reagan in the United States, will have the flexibility that Roosevelt, Kennedy, or Johnson possessed. Political leadership, post-Reagan, and independently of party, must confront a citizenry that will remain sceptical of political nostrums and that will attribute special-interest motivations to any and all political agents. This public scepticism will be added on to the fiscal constraints already noted. The challenge to be faced by any prospective political leader in the post-Reagan years is immense.

5   Rent-seekers versus Constitutionalists

I suggested above (p. 2) that the post-Reagan political economy in America will be described by the struggle between the rent-seekers and the constitutionalists, and that almost all citizens will play, simultaneously, both of these rôles. If we understand modern democratic politics in these terms, we remain within realistic models and steer clear of engaging in romantic images. Each of us will seek to utilise the political process to further the privately determined and specialised interest that affects us most directly, either through providing us with desired, positively-valued activities from which we secure benefits or through preventing negatively valued actions from being carried out to our cost. In this use of the political process we are rent-seekers, and I use this term to refer to any sought-for objective that involves concentrated benefits or costs.

If I seek a special tax exemption for my industry, my profession, my region, I am rent-seeking. If I seek a special spending programme that will benefit my pet project, whether this will provide me with personal pecuniary gain or not, I am rent-seeking. I am seeking to secure *differential* gains that are not shared by the full constituency. In game theory terms, I am behaving non-co-operatively; I am engaging in politics treated as a non-co-operative game. To the extent that politics may be accurately regarded as a competitive struggle among the rent-seekers, it will, in total, be negative sum, or, at best, zero sum – that is to say, the aggregate losses will be larger than the aggregate gains.

A negative-sum game

If this is all there is to politics, if all, or almost all, members of the polity consider themselves to wind up as net losers, despite the differential gains that may be secured from favourable political action on their favoured programme, pressures will increase to change the rules. Why will rational persons continue to play in a negative-sum game and, further, negative sum over all, or almost all, participants? If this result should be characteristic of a game in which persons voluntarily participate, the game could not survive. Players would, quite simply, leave the game. In this sense, it is improper to model politics by analogy with voluntary games. Individual members of a political community cannot readily exercise an exit option, especially at the level of the national political unit. If emigration thresholds are high, individuals must change the rules as an alternative to leaving the game itself.

In taking action to change the rules of the political game, based on the recognition that the rent-seeking struggle takes place within the existing rules, the individual behaves as a constitutionalist. I have suggested that, within each of us, there is a conflict between our political behaviour as a rent-seeker and our political behaviour as a constitutionalist.

Rising above interest groups

In a paper delivered at the American Economic Association meetings in Chicago in December 1987, William Niskanen, former member of Reagan's Council of Economic Advisors, pointed to three separate political events in the United States that seem to reflect the constitutionalist element at work in the political process, the element that is basically co-operative rather than conflictual.[2] He pointed to the whole deregulation movement, to the tax reform legislation of 1986, and to the Gramm–Rudman–Hollings budgetary constraints, enacted first in 1985 and revised in 1987. In each of these cases, the beneficiaries seem to be the citizenry generally rather than concentrated interest groups. As Niskanen suggested, the political economist who tries to remain with a rent-seeking model of democratic politics cannot explain these events. These events can be satisfactorily understood only when it is recognised that a constitutionalist model, which directs attention towards effective changes in rules that will benefit all, or almost all, players, also explains at least some aspects of observed political reality.

As I have noted earlier, the distinguishing feature of the post-Reagan political economy will be that the struggle between the rent-seeking special interests and the constitutionalist effort to secure general benefits from changes in rules, will be carried on without the romantic delusion that political agents seek to further some general or 'public interest', or, indeed, that any such interest exists. Before the 1960s, this delusion was omnipresent in all discussions about and attitudes towards politics and politicians. And it was this delusion that enabled many special-interest programmes involving concentrated benefits to be approved unwittingly by the electorate. Because these programmes are now established, as a part of the post-Reagan *status quo*, we cannot predict wholesale dismantling, even if the error in initial politicisation comes to be widely acknowledged. We can, however, predict that, without the romance of the public interest, or of the genuinely benevolent state, special benefits to concentrated interests will be more difficult to implement through the political process. Can we expect to see more Tulsa or Tombigbee canals, both notorious examples of American 'pork-barrel' spending, in the 1990s?

Binding constraints

Let me be a bit more specific about the supergame involving the rent-seekers and the constitutionalists in particular areas of policy and politics. There is perhaps a better recognition of the negative-sum aspects of the spending–taxing–deficit process, as carried on by both the Reagan presidency and the Congress in the 1980s, than for other areas of policy. The Gramm–Rudman–Hollings legislation, although not so desirable from a constitutionalist perspective as an amendment to the United States' written constitution would be, nonetheless reflects a recognition by the Congress that its spending rules, its procedures, were out of hand and that binding constraints are required. The test for the post-Reagan years will be whether or not the discipline signalled by the Gramm–Rudman–Hollings legislation, and by the attempts to work within its discipline, will carry over beyond 1991.

The issue on which there does not seem to be adequate recognition for the necessity to operate within general rules that constrain political rent-seeking is that of trade policy. Potentially, the post-Reagan political economy seems most vulnerable to the protectionist urgings of special-interest groups which may, through a set of logrolled political exchanges, succeed in imposing major damage on the national economy. We could find our incomes reduced in post-Reagan years if we allow legislation to be enacted that will close up our markets. This threat can be contained and offset only if the citizenry, and its political agents, recognise the self-defeating or negative-sum aspect of the protectionist argument. The constitutionalist position here is that which was taken by Cordell Hull in the 1930s; trade policy, industry-by-industry, cannot effectively be made by Congress, which necessarily allows for complex trade-offs among separate beneficiary groups to the damage of the general electorate.

6 Constitutional Democracy

Any description of the American political economy, post-Reagan, must be informed by an understanding of what the American polity is and how it differs from other national polities. The United States is a republic; there is a written constitution, a two-house legislature, an executive with veto powers, and a supreme court with authority for review. This political régime is different in many respects from the idealised parliamentary democracy, which is much closer to the majoritarian model of collective decision-making so favoured by political scientists. Majority coalitions in the USA are much more constrained in what they can do and the speed with which they can do it than are parliamentary régimes. This difference alone is, I think, sufficient to explain why the American economy came to be somewhat *less* politicised over the century when politics was viewed romantically than those other Western economies, including the United Kingdom, where majoritarian dominance was characteristic. But this difference also explains why Mrs Thatcher has been more successful than Ronald Reagan in carrying through on pledges and promises for effective depoliticisation. Parliamentary régimes depend relatively more on who is in office and relatively less on the incentive structure facing whoever is in elective office. Put very simply, a constitutional democracy is constitutional, which means that rules matter.

The President's opportunity

This difference in structure is important in understanding my overall theme for this paper. Let me return to the supergame involving rent-seeking competition on the one hand and constitutional efforts to change the rules on the other. By the nature of the structure, special-interest coalitions tend to find their initial support in the US Congress, which is organised, deliberately, on the basis of dispersed geographical representation. Congressional dominance of the executive necessarily implies that relatively more political rent-seeking will take place with relatively less constitutional thrust. By contrast, because the President is representative of the whole electorate, there is, in the presidency, a 'natural' location for attention to genuinely constitutional approaches to policy reform. It is in this sense that I judge the Reagan presidency to have failed; it paid too little attention to structure and it seems to have been too interested in playing the policy-within-politics game, too interested in pushing its policy agenda within a relatively short time perspective.

What can we predict for post-Reagan politics? Quite independently of the electoral results, because of the constitutional structure itself we can predict reasonable stability in policy. There can be no dramatic reversals in trend. Indeed, 1933 was perhaps unique to US history in that this was a peacetime year when dramatic change was possible. A post-Reagan president can adopt a constitutionalist stance and consider proposing changes in the rules that will effectively constrain the rent-seekers. The opportunity for this position to be successful will not, however, be that faced by Ronald Reagan in 1980. Quite apart from prospects for success, there seems little likelihood that the new President will adopt even so partial a constitutionalist stance as Reagan did in 1980. If policy-within-politics ultimately came to dominate the Reagan years, we can scarcely expect the post-Reagan president to place structural change high on his attention listing.

Mutual exploitation or rule change

Hard-headed and sober predictions about the post-Reagan years suggest that we will witness relatively more negative-sum rent-seeking through the agencies of national politics. These predictions are tempered somewhat when we recognise the total absence of any supportive romantic image of governmental benevolence. Can the rent-seekers continue to engage in mutual exploitation through politics without some myth of public interest? My own romantic prediction, based largely on hope rather than analysis, is that the time will be ripe for intellectual entrepreneurs in particular to convey the constitutionalist message. This message is simple and does not urge persons to act contrary to their interests. Changing rules can be, and is, in the interests of *all* the players, especially as they are caught up in the competitive struggle among interest groups, each of which exploits all others. Personally, I think I have a moral obligation to believe that we can move towards a restoration of the vision of James Madison.

7 Post-election Postscript

The substantial election victory of George Bush confirms my hypothesis that the romance between the American electorate and the state has faded into near-oblivion. Even if somewhat lukewarmly proffered, Governor Dukakis did call for an extension and expansion of the political domain of the federal government. The accompanying electoral successes of the Democrats in both houses of the Congress confirmed another hypothesis concerning the increasing importance of rent-seeking, special-interest politics. Members of Congress act in furtherance of the interests of defined constituencies, and one of President Bush's major problems will be to control the excesses that coalitions of special-interest groups will seek to enact.

Protectionist legislation, additional to that which is already embodied in the 1988 trade bill, will move through Congress. George Bush and James Baker seem to understand the logic of free trade, but whether their expected rhetoric will be matched by effective control of protectionist pressures is not predictable. More generally, there is no indication that George Bush thinks and acts on the basis of *constitutional principle* even to the extent that motivated Ronald Reagan.

Bush deliberately locked himself into a no-tax-increase position in his campaign commitments. He will succeed in holding off tax-rate increases if costs under Medicare can be reasonably contained, and if new spending initiatives are kept in check. The payroll tax increases enacted in 1983 are beginning to accumulate surpluses in the social security account, and these surpluses act to make the budget deficit, overall, seem less than independent accounting would suggest. The Gramm–Rudman targets for reduction in the size of the comprehensive deficit can be met under favourable economic conditions, even if the problems of funding future commitments to retirees are exacerbated.

The most severe threat to economic policy in the Bush presidency may stem from a possible financial crisis, triggered by collapse of saving and loan units, or by foreign debtors. If, in response to such crises, the Federal

Reserve authority responds with increases in liquidity, inflationary pressures will accelerate, with rapidly shifting expectations. This inflation would, in turn, prompt monetary restrictions which would generate recession. This scenario need not occur, but the fragility, and hence nonpredictability, of the whole set of complex monetary arrangements, both domestic and international, ought to be emphasised.

There is little or no evidence that a Bush–Baker–Brady administration will understand or seek *constitutional* approaches to the resolution of the issues of political economy that must surely emerge in the 1989–93 years.

Notes

1 Robert Higgs's book, *Crisis and Leviathan*, Oxford University Press, New York, 1986, provides a good source for the material sketched out here.
2 William Niskanen, 'The Political Economy of Gramm–Rudman and other "Policy Accidents"', unpublished manuscript, Cato Institute, Washington DC, 1987.

2

An American Perspective: from 'Markets Work to Public Choice'

with Gordon Tullock

1 Introduction

We have been careful to entitle this paper 'An American Perspective' rather than anything more general. In the initial invitation, we were asked to discuss the Institute of Economic Affairs as viewed by American 'public-choice economists', an invitation that in itself suggested the restrictiveness of our vantage point. While we do hope to discuss the IEA in a somewhat wider context than that of 'public choice', narrowly conceived, we make no claim to represent mainstream or orthodox American attitudes, to reflect 'establishment' opinion, whether reserved for the limited group of applied economists or extended to describe the intelligentsia.

Decisions and institutions

In the first of these settings, that of applied economics (often labelled as 'public policy'), we are perhaps somewhat less sympathetic to the main thrust of the IEA's efforts over the quarter-century than those of our American counterparts who have, in their own researches, paralleled the IEA thrust more closely. In a real sense, 'public-choice' research is more 'institutional' than straightforward applied economics. 'Public choice' examines more carefully the political, or government and bureaucratic structures, rules, and procedures (the *institutions*) through which policy

Published originally as a contribution to *The Emerging Consensus? Essays on the Interplay Between Ideas, Interests and Circumstances in the First 25 Years of the IEA* (1981).

decisions are made, and less the *content* of the decisions themselves.

Having said this, however, we should hasten to add, indeed to emphasise, that it is through the IEA's efforts that public-choice research has been brought to the attention of the academic–intellectual–journalistic community in Great Britain. These efforts were expressed particularly in the IEA's 1978 and 1979 symposia on the 'economics of politics', in which both of us participated,[1] and in the publication of several of our works, along with those of others who represent public choice, broadly defined.[2] There is, indeed there must be, a close relationship between constructive research in applied economics (or public policy) and in public choice, the 'science' or sub-discipline that examines more directly the means through which policy programmes are chosen and implemented.

The market works

In six words or less, what has been the thrust of the IEA's research programme? 'The market alternative works'. This has been the central hypothesis of most of the IEA's efforts in positive economic analysis (of what *is*). The demonstration of the validity of this hypothesis, in one industry, occupation or other application after another, has, in a more or less natural progression, allowed the normative imperative (of what *should be* done – policy) often to be stated as: 'Try the market', or, even more concisely if with some apologies to the Queen's English, 'privatise'.[3]

Comparably, the thrust of the research programme in public choice may be somewhat sketchily put as: 'The governmental–political alternative does not work'. Research in public choice has concentrated on the way government functions. As a result it has been discovered that commonly *the government alternative is inherently inferior to the market*. There have been two positive implications, one of which is to shift much government activity to the market and the other is to change government structure so as to improve its efficiency. The central 'government fails' hypothesis, again in numerous applications in IEA papers, has been demonstrated in positive analysis of varying degrees of analytical rigour. Again, given the analytical support of the hypothesis, the conclusion for policy often becomes: 'Try the market' or 'Privatise.'

The change in policy

The two research themes seem to converge, therefore, at the level of the normative implication of what should be done. There remains a difference, however, and one that deserves some discussion. The imperative, as stated briefly, may be directed differently. The central message may be aimed at the attitudes of political leaders, in party councils or legislative chambers, and at the supporting attitudes of the general public. The implementation of the imperative involves a shift in attitudes followed by an explicit *change in policy*.

Council houses, for example, are sold; airlines are de-regulated. By comparison with this more direct approach to desired policy shifts, public choice aims its message at the institutional structure through which policy is made and changed. It aims at more comprehensive, and long range, reform as opposed to piecemeal, pragmatic change. Public choice, in its normative dress, suggests that mere shifts in policy are likely to be temporary, and that effective reform lies only in a modification of the rules that allow legislatures to enact good (or bad) policy. With a well-designed legislature the kind of error which involves detailed interference with the ordinary workings of the market should be much less likely than with current structures. Further, constitutional limitations on such intervention may be desirable, although here the possibility that the constitution can always be changed puts limits on what can be done. This structural reform involves much more than the limited claim that enlightened politicians should not enact legislation involving such detailed interference with the working of markets.

2 The Transmission of Ideas

The whole set of questions concerning the transmission of ideas, particularly those with potential political impact, is highly important. Unfortunately, we know relatively little here. The only reasonably rigorous model for idea transmission through society is a direct transcription of the theory of contagious diseases developed by medical scientists. The resemblance between a contagious disease and the spread of an idea may not be immediately obvious, although perhaps many would regard the analogy as helpful in explaining the spread of Marxism. The similarity, however, is in practice quite strong. In both, a person who has a particular germ or a particular idea contacts someone else and either does or does not transmit the germ or idea. Whether the disease or idea spreads throughout the population depends on the frequency of contact and the ease with which it may be transmitted.

In both contagious diseases and ideas there may be means of transmission other than direct person-to-person contact. A germ or an idea may lie dormant for considerable periods (the idea in a forgotten book in the library) and then be picked up and begin to spread. Further, there exist mechanisms for what you might call mass transmission: a city water supply for disease or the mass media for an idea. Unfortunately the mathematical model of transmission is very hard to use, even in the contagious diseases where it was invented. It would be even more difficult to 'model' the spread of ideas. Mathematically the two processes might perhaps be treated as mappings of each other, but this correspondence may be of little help granted that the mathematics is apparently much too difficult for practical application in either case.

In human society ideas not only have to be spread; they also have to be invented. In this respect there is a difference between public choice and the IEA. The Institute has mainly devoted itself to spreading ideas that were in existence. Public choice, on the other hand, has been more concerned with inventing new ideas, or, at the least, the discovery of new applications for established methods of analysis. We should not over-simplify here, and we do not want to stress the contrast. The IEA has, of course, been responsible for the development of original ideas, and public choice has included considerable effort to spreading ideas already in existence. Nonetheless, and by its own acknowledgement, the Institute to a large extent has devoted itself to the propagation of ideas that have been in existence for quite a long time, but which had been largely forgotten. The development of new ideas, particularly new applications of neo-classical economics, has increasingly become an important aspect of the Institute's work, but, over the quarter-century, this has remained considerably less important than the spreading of old, valid but neglected ideas.

3 Public Choice and the IEA: Temporal Cohorts

The Institute is what it says it is: an institute that is physically located in London, with influence that extends over Great Britain and many other countries. It may seem folly to attempt any comparison of an 'Institute' with what can be best called a 'sub-discipline', *public choice*, which as such is not located at any place,[4] and which is described best as a method of research. Such a comparison is not quite the apples and oranges that it may seem, however, when we recognise that the IEA and public choice are temporal cohorts. Both have emerged full grown in the quarter-century spanned by the mid-1950s and the early 1980s. The research emphasis, both of the Institute and of public choice, reflects a reaction against that of mainstream economics over the period. Keynesian macro-economics was still in its phase of delusionary grandeur in the middle 1950s,[5] when both were founded.

Neglect of micro-economics

In late 1980, it is hard to remember the situation at the time the IEA was founded. Even in the United States, where the situation was not so extreme as in Britain, micro-economics had been substantially replaced by macro-economics as the active field for applied economic policy. The situation was perhaps unique in history. Most economists had, of course, studied micro-economics and courses in it continued to be taught. Indeed, early editions of Samuelson's textbook, *Economics*, devoted about half of their pages to micro-economics. And articles on micro-economic problems continued to be published in the economic literature.

Nevertheless, in a real sense, micro-economics was largely forgotten. The existing frontier was macro-economics. Government policy advisers in the USA and Britain hardly ever turned their attention from macro-economic questions. (In the United States, a partial exception was present in the work of economists in the Rand Foundation who commenced work in defence economics.) Samuelson's textbook, although half micro-economics, presented the macro-economics first, and presumably many teachers of elementary economics never got around to the 'tedious' chapters on micro-economics.

All of this has, of course, changed since the 1960s. In part the change came simply because the macro-economic models do not seem to fit the present-day world. In part it came because economic advisers began to get nervous about offering any kind of macro advice. (On one recent occasion in a meeting of the American Economic Association, Gordon Tullock asked Robert Solow what advice could be given to President Carter. Solow, a leading Keynesian macro-economist replied, 'I sympathise with your question.')

Micro-economics probably remained largely unknown to many of the post-1950s economists who were trained in the post-war years. They may have been compelled to take micro-economics courses, but both they and their instructors thought of this analysis as some rather tedious bit of history of the discipline, more or less like Latin. Even for those who learned the lessons, there was little or no interest in applications. The whole policy literature was dominated by Keynesians, or by economists whose political positions suggested that Keynesian methods and tools were more appropriate to their purposes.

Breakdown of communications

There were, of course, many scholars, both economists and scholars in other fields, who still remembered the older ideas. But communication among them had broken down. They tended to be isolated individuals in clusters of one or two at particular universities and there was very little interaction among them, in part because the orthodoxy was so much dominated by the opposing policy thrust. Those who sensed that there was something wrong with the then-prevailing macro-economic orthodoxy, but who themselves did not have a background in classical economics at all, were even more unfortunate. They tended to be critics who did not themselves have anything in the way of a coherent position of their own. These critics of the existing system felt cut off and isolated, and willing to turn to almost any expedient. But they were not capable of developing a coherent counter-position simply because of the breakdown in communication.

The situation in Britain was in many ways worse than in the United States, and when Antony Fisher founded and Ralph Harris and Arthur Seldon developed the Institute of Economic Affairs, they may well have thought of themselves as voices crying in the wilderness. However, they had much to build on. The halcyon days of classical political economy had not been wholly forgotten, and there were many individuals who were still interested in the neo-classical economics of Marshall. A first step was to put these scholars in better communication with one another by providing a format for publication, which would at the same time have the effect of transmitting the ideas to a wider audience. The Institute could and did both stimulate research and development of a coherent point of view by permitting the existing scholars with a pro-market approach to communicate with one another and at the same time provide for their ideas to be more widely disseminated.

The escapist mathematical priesthood

By contrast with the origins of the IEA, public choice did not emerge specifically as a reaction against a macro-policy emphasis. Its origins were based on a somewhat more general reaction against the pervasive neglect by economists (and political scientists) of the political–governmental *institutions* through which any policy, micro or macro, must be implemented. Both the IEA and public choice have served as counterweights to the proclivity of modern economists to engage themselves predominantly in escapist mathematical rigour, spurred by some apparent effort to create a priesthood defined by an ability to communicate one with another in a language inaccessible to all non-members.

The counterweight objectives have been successful to a degree; the apogee of formalism[6] in economic theory has been reached, and its most skilful practitioners now turn their minds to the sobering reality of the world as it exists. In this respect, the IEA, perhaps largely due to the editorial persuasiveness of Arthur Seldon, has been more successful than public choice. In the latter, the mathematical properties of some of the complex collective choice problems have proved too tempting to the prospective priests, and there has been no Arthur Seldon to ride herd over a rapidly growing sub-discipline.

4 Ideas, Education, and Literature

The IEA's very successful rôle in the transmission of 'market works' ideas took two forms. The first and most conspicuous is, of course, the very well worked out dissemination activity carried on by the Institute. No one who has ever had lunch at Eaton Square or Lord North Street can fail to be impressed with the Institute's ability to penetrate the 'establishment' of Britain. But the success of 1981 in these respects is built on hard work in days when the IEA was not so conspicuous as it now appears. Indispensable for the successful public relations activity was the development of a body of literature which countered the then-dominant conventional wisdom.

A student in Oxford who might have been assigned a paper on some government policy would have found some difficulty in obtaining economic analysis outside the prevailing Keynesian-benevolent despot orthodoxy before the IEA's list. All of this changed with the Institute's steady and respected series of publications, first from Hobart Place, then

Eaton Square, then Lord North Street. With time, over the quarter-century, the development of a battery of publications by the IEA covering substantially all policy matters provided a firm intellectual basis for opposition to the collectivist orthodoxy. Further, this set of publications provided an indispensable base for the more direct educational activities. These, of course, have far more immediate impact on policy. In the long run, however, the publication series may have had even more impact through its influence on the younger generation of scholars and then through them eventually on the public.

It should not be forgotten, however, that the efforts in education and publicity have a somewhat similar long-range effect. An individual politician, civil servant, or even journalist, who is introduced to an unorthodox point of view is likely to continue for a very long period to remain aware of the existence of such unorthodox points of view and willing to pay attention to them. He may indeed be converted, with the result that there is a long-range effect there too. Further, the educational activity no doubt had a good deal to do with the fact that the scholarly publications attracted a fairly wide readership. As authors of several IEA papers we should like to feel that the widespread press attention they got simply reflected their merit. But we cannot fail to notice that when we publish under other auspices, and especially in the United States, we do not get nearly so much general public attention.

As we noted in 2, the process of spreading ideas through society is not well understood. It is not possible to say for certain that the quite significant change in economic attitudes in Britain over the quarter-century is the result of IEA activities. We can say for certain that it is not solely the result of the Institute. Nonetheless, the Institute has found what appears to be a sensible and successful strategy. It involves a well-organised combination of scholarly publications and public dissemination which has proved successful, made so in part by the skill and devotion of the people in the IEA, but also in part because of the special nature of British society over the quarter-century.

If, however, the intellectual climate in Britain is radically different in 1981 from the one that existed when the IEA was founded, this does not imply that the IEA has won a war. What we really should say is that the first skirmishes have gone very well. The major battle is not yet won, but it would seem sensible to continue with the same general strategy.

5 Why no American IEA?

It has long been common among American friends of the IEA to ask ourselves why no comparable institution exists in the United States. Some attempt to answer such a question can perhaps indicate something of our own American perspective.

At the outset, we shall state categorically that we are pleased that the IEA does not, and cannot, have an American equivalent. We state this while at the same time we should emphasise that, were we British citizens, we should indeed value highly the net contribution of the IEA. Most simply put, the United States has no IEA because it has no London. Despite its claims to emergence as the national cultural centre, and despite the horrendous growth of the bureaucracy, Washington, even in the early 1980s, remains a closer relative to Canberra or Brasilia than it does to London. We should have to imagine New York, Boston, Washington, Chicago, New Orleans, Los Angeles, and San Francisco rolled into one to create some United States analogue to London.

Why is this geographical dispersal relevant in examining the potential for an American equivalent of the IEA? The IEA has remained at the centre of the British establishment, whether intellectually, culturally, commercially, or politically defined, but, at the same time, it has not been 'captured' by the establishment. This somewhat peculiar, but highly productive, stance would not have been possible in Washington, even with the devotion, wisdom, and integrity of Ralph Harris and Arthur Seldon. Transplanted onto the District of Columbia turf, the IEA would have, we venture to suggest, become at least partially captured by the pressure-backed political–legislative–bureaucracy jungle, and hence largely incapable of exhibiting the long-range coherence of purpose that has been its London hallmark.

6 Constitutional Reform, Public Choice, and the IEA in 2006

When the IEA commenced operation in 1957, its argument to the effect that 'the market alternative works' was not directly in the mainstream of current economic policy discussion in Britain. In the setting of that time, this argument was indeed 'way out', a facet of history that is difficult even for us who lived through it to recall. The quarter-century has been characterised by a catching-up, by a dwindling distance between the concerns of the IEA and the concerns of those 'experts' who offer advice and counsel on economic affairs of the day, on *current policy*. As we indicated above, the war of ideas has by no means been won on the ways in which economic policy is shaped and directed. And surely the IEA's challenges in these more or less traditional areas of emphasis remain large.

Constitutional reform: a leap forward

At the same time, however, the IEA should make efforts to 'leap forward', to establish or re-establish some considerable distance between some of its research focus and that of the economic policy politics of the 1980s. And, to those of us who work in *constitutional* analysis and design, the IEA's expressed interests in public choice in 1978 and 1979 are highly encouraging. This shift of emphasis suggests to us that, over the next quarter-century, the events of politics may later be described as a 'catching up' with ideas of those 'academic scribblers'[7] who now talk about basic constitutional change, about reform in the structure of political order.

As with the 'markets work' argument of the mid-1950s, the 'constitutional reform' argument of the 1980s will be, and will be seen to be, somewhat remote from the expressed concerns of current policy advocates. But public choice, in its positive aspects, has taught us that policy programmes emerge from and are directly influenced by the structure of the institutions through which decisions are made.

Teaching the lessons of elementary micro-economics, elementary price theory, to separate generations of elected or potentially elected public leaders will, of course, remain a noble cause. But it will remain folly to rely on the ignorance and illiteracy of past and present politicians as the only source of hope for a better record of achievement over the second quarter-century of the IEA's history. Political leaders, along with those who support them, deserve to be examined and analysed as everyone else, with enough insight to understand their individual interests, broadly defined. But if this minimal step is taken towards re-interpretation, attention is necessarily drawn to the structure of the institutions, and to the incentives, the rewards and penalties, for the persons who act within the constraints of such institutions. Do the potential leaders really need the lessons of elementary economics so much as to be allowed to act within a reformed structure of institutions.

Unfortunately, perhaps, there is no ready-made discipline to draw on in constitutional analysis that is remotely comparable to that of classical and neo-classical political economy. The 'markets work' argument was an application of an established discipline, even if sometimes forgotten in the Keynesian delusion. But things are different when we come to discuss constitutional reform. Orthodox political science or government, as an academic discipline, offers little here. But the wisdom of the 18th century can be re-evaluated, and it can come to inform the minds of modern men. The 18th-century scepticism about the abilities of politics, of government, to handle detailed regulatory tasks, to go beyond the limits of the 'minimal' or 'protection' state, is an attitude of mind that is capable of attainment.

A radical challenge to the IEA

What specific steps might be taken by the IEA in the early 1980s that would ensure progress in the direction indicated, over and beyond the acknowledged interest in and promotion of understanding and application of public choice? The importance and relevance of political and legal philosophy must be recognised. Comparative research on alternative constitutional and governmental structures can be encouraged. The work of economists and other scholars who have managed to remove 'majoritarian parliamentary democracy' from the realm of the sacrosanct can be published.

In sum, it is time for the IEA, in part at least, to become *radical*, in the literal meaning of this term, to seek out and explore the ultimate sources of social order. The 'markets work' ideas promulgated by the IEA from 1957 were radical in the intellectual setting of the Britain of that time. These ideas have now become topical currency. Our plea is for the IEA to invest some of its resources in making a new leap forward, to shift dramatically beyond the boundaries directly relevant to policy, to encourage and sponsor research and discussion of constitutional structures that may seem fixed in concrete to orthodox mentalities. So conceived, the challenge for the second quarter-century can be equally important and equally exciting as that for the first.

Notes

1 *The Economics of Politics*, IEA Readings 18, 1978, and *The Taming of Government*, IEA Readings 21, 1979.
2 Gordon Tullock, *The Vote Motive*, Hobart Paperback 9, 1976; J. M. Buchanan, R. E. Wagner and John Burton, *The Consequences of Mr Keynes*, Hobart Paper 78, 1978; W. A. Niskanen, *Bureaucracy: Servant or Master?*, Hobart Paperback 5, 1973.
3 [Or, even more colloquially, 'suck it and see'. – Ed.]
4 Although we like to think that our own Center for Study of Public Choice at Virginia Polytechnic Institute does offer a locational focus for the more inclusive effort.
5 'Economic policy in immediate post-war decades was dominated by the writings of John Maynard Keynes. An almost idolatrous adoration surrounded him.' (Lord Balogh, 'Is Keynes Dead?', *New Republic*, 7 June 1980, pp. 15–18.)
6 [Formalism in macro-economics was analysed by Professor L. M. Lachmann in *Macro-economic Thinking and the Market Economy*, Hobart Paper 56, IEA, 1973. – Ed.]
7 [The source of this famous phrase is, of course, J. M. Keynes, *The General Theory of Employment, Interest and Money*, Macmillan, 1936, p. 383. – Ed.]

3

From Private Preferences to Public Philosophy: the Development of Public Choice

1 Introduction

I appreciate the opportunity afforded me by this invitation from the Institute of Economic Affairs to come to London and to open this seminar on the 'Economics of Politics', or as we prefer to call it in the US, 'Public Choice', which is really the application and extension of economic theory to the realm of political or governmental choices. I shall be talking here about material that is familiar to many of you, but it remains nonetheless true that 'public-choice' has been somewhat slower to attract attention in the United Kingdom than elsewhere in Europe. This body of ideas has been relatively neglected here, despite the presence of one of the genuinely seminal scholars in the discipline, Duncan Black, who has been, in one sense, a prophet without honour in his own country, or at least without appropriate honour.

I shall return to the position of 'public choice' in the UK, but first let me say that the sub-discipline is currently thriving, not only in America, but in West Germany, in Switzerland, in Japan, and, most recently, in

Published originally as a contribution to IEA Readings No. 18, *The Economics of Politics* (1978). Basic reference works in public choice are listed at the end of the chapter. A more sophisticated survey of the discipline is in Dennis C. Mueller, 'Public Choice: A Survey', *Journal of Economic Literature*, Vol. 14, No. 2 (June 1976), pp. 395–433. This survey paper is followed by Mueller's longer monograph, *Public Choice*, Cambridge University Press, 1979. My survey paper, 'Public Finance and Public Choice', *National Tax Journal*, December 1975, relates developments in public choice to public finance. An elementary treatment of the various topics in public choice theory will be found in Gordon Tullock, *The Vote Motive*, Hobart Paperback No. 9, IEA (1976).

France, where Henri Lepage has recently published a laudatory descriptive essay in *Réalités* (November 1977), an expanded version of which has now appeared as a chapter in Lepage's fascinating book *Demain le capitalisme* (1978).

History of neglect of 'public choice' in the UK

The relative neglect of 'public choice' in the UK is traceable to factors that extend back for two centuries. To the classical economists, the state was unproductive. As a result of this common presupposition, less attention was paid to the analysis of state activity. Britain was also the origin of Benthamite utilitarianism, which provided idealised objectives for governmental policy to the neglect of institutional structure. Britain was also the home of idealist political philosophy in the late-19th century, a philosophy that put up barriers against any realistic examination of politics. Finally, the very dominance of Britain in the theory of the private economy, through the major influence of Alfred Marshall, drew intellectual resources away from the theory of the public economy. British and American analysis in public finance was a half-century out of date by the onset of World War II; the seminal contributions of the Continental scholars at the turn of the century and before were largely ignored, notably those of the outstanding Swedish economist, Knut Wicksell.

In Britain, you surely hold on longer than most people to the romantic notion that government seeks only to do good in some hazily defined Benthamite sense, and, furthermore, to the hypothesis that government could, in fact, accomplish most of what it set out to do.

Your economists, and notably Lord Keynes, along with their American counterparts, continued to proffer policy advice as if they were talking to a benevolent despot who stood at their beck and call.[1] This despite Wicksell's clear but simple warning in 1896 that economic policy is made by politicians who are participants in a legislative process, and that economists could not ignore these elementary facts. But British and American economists throughout most of this century continued to seem blind to what now appears so simple to us, that benevolent despots do not exist and that governmental policy emerges from a highly complex and intricate institutional structure peopled by ordinary men and women, very little different from the rest of us. The political scientists were, if anything, even more naïve than the economists, and they have not, even today, learned very much.

2 The Economic Theory of Politics

Why do we call our sub-discipline the 'economic' theory of politics? What is there that is peculiarly 'economic' about it? Here I think we can look to Duncan Black to put us on the right track. Black commenced his work by stating, very simply, that for his analysis an individual is nothing more than a set of preferences, a utility function, as we call it. Once this apparently innocent definition of an individual is accepted, you are really trapped. If you are to argue that individuals have *similar* preferences, you are forced into a position where you must explain why. And if you can think of no good reason why they should do so, you are required to acknowledge that preferences may *differ* among persons.

From these innocent beginnings, the economic theory of politics emerges as a matter of course. The theory is 'economic' in the sense that, like traditional economic theory, the building blocks are *individuals*, not corporate entities, not societies, not communities, not states. The building blocks are living, choosing, economising persons. If these persons are allowed to have *differing* preferences, and if we so much as acknowledge that some aspects of life are inherently collective or social rather than purely private, the central problem for public choice jumps at you full blown. How are differing individual preferences to be reconciled in reaching results that must, by definition, be shared jointly by all members of the community? The positive question is: How *are* the differences reconciled under the political institutions we observe? This question is accompanied by the normative one: How *should* the differences among individuals in desired results be reconciled?

Even at this most elementary level, we must examine the purpose of the collectivity. I have often contrasted the 'economic' approach to politics with what I have called the 'truth judgement' approach. Individuals may differ on their judgements as to what is 'true' and what is not, and it is possible that, occasionally, we may want to introduce institutions that essentially collect or poll the opinions of several persons in arriving at some best estimate of what is 'true' or 'right'. The jury comes to mind as the best example here. The accused is either guilty or not guilty, and we use the jury to determine which of these judgements is 'true'. But for matters of ordinary politics, the question is *not* one of truth and falsity of the alternatives. The problem is one of resolving individual differences of preferences into results, which it is misleading to call true or false.

We can return to the parallel with standard economic theory. A result emerges from a process of exchange, of compromise, of mutual adjustment among several persons, each of whom has private preferences over the alternatives. Further, the satisfaction of these private preferences offers the *raison d'être* for collective action in the first place. The membership of a congregation decides, somehow, that the church-house is to be painted blue rather than green, but it is inappropriate to talk of either colour as being 'true'. The members of a school board decide to hire Mr Jones rather than Mr Brown, but we can scarcely say that the successful candidate embodies 'truth'.

The paradox of voting

Let me return to Duncan Black's seminal efforts, as he faced up to the central problem. I am sure that the natural starting place for Black was with ordinary committees that are used to govern many kinds of collective activities. In this, Black was probably influenced by his own participation in the machinery used for making university-college decisions, much as Lewis Carroll had been influenced by his own share in the committee governance of Christ Church, Oxford. And it is through Duncan Black that we know that the UK's claim to early ideas in voting theory rest largely with Lewis Carroll, who joins the French nobleman, Condorcet, in making up the two most important figures in the 'history of doctrine' before the middle years of this century.

How do committees reach decisions when agreement among all members is not possible? Simple observation suggested the relevance of analysing simple majority voting in formal terms. When he carried out this analysis Black was, I think, somewhat disappointed, even if not surprised, to find that there may exist no motion or proposal (or candidate) from among a fixed set of possibilities that will defeat all others in a series of one-against-one majority tests. There may exist no majority motion. If this is the case, simple majority voting will produce continuous cycling or rotation among a subgroup or subset of the available alternatives. The collective outcome will depend on where the voting stops, which will, in turn, depend on the manipulation of the agenda as well as upon the rules of order. The committee member who can ensure that his preferred amendment or motion is voted upon just before adjournment often wins the strategic game that majority rules always introduce. (It is interesting, even today, to observe the reactions of fellow committee members when a public choice economist observes that the outcome of deliberation may well be dependent on the voting rules adopted.) The 'paradox of voting' became one of the staple ingredients in any subsequent public-choice discourse.

Arrow's 'paradox of social (collective) choice'

Only a short time after Black's early efforts, Kenneth Arrow (Nobel Laureate in Economics, now of Harvard University) confronted a somewhat different and more general problem, although he was to reach the same conclusion. Arrow tried to construct what some economists call a 'social welfare function' designed to be useful in guiding the planning authority for a society. He sought to do so by amalgamating information about the separate preferences of individual members, and he was willing to assume that the individuals' preferences exhibit the standard properties required for persons to make ordinary market choices. To his surprise, Arrow found that no such 'social welfare function' could be constructed; the task was a logical impossibility, given the satisfaction of certain plausible side-conditions. The paradox of voting became the more general and more serious paradox of social or collective choice.

Perhaps it is unfair to both, but I think that Duncan Black would have been happier if he could have discovered that majority voting rules do produce consistent outcomes, and that Kenneth Arrow would have been happier if he could have been able to demonstrate that a social welfare function could be constructed. Black was, and to my knowledge remains, dedicated to government by majority rule; Arrow was, and to my knowledge remains, an advocate of social planning. Black started immediately to look for the set of conditions that preferences must meet in order for majority voting to exhibit consistency. He came up with his notion of 'single-peakedness' which means that if all individual preferences among alternatives can be arrayed along a single dimension so that there is a single peak for each voter, there will exist a unique majority motion or proposal (or candidate). This alternative will be that one of the available sets of proposals that is most preferred by the median voter. In this setting, majority voting does produce a definitive result, and in so doing it satisfies voters in the middle more than voters at either extreme. For example, if voters on school budgets can be divided roughly into three groups of comparable size – big spenders, medium spenders, and low spenders – the medium spenders will be controlling under ordinary majority voting, provided that neither the low nor the high spenders rank medium spending lowest among the three budget options. The formal collective or social choice theorists, shocked by the Arrow impossibility theorem, have continued to try to examine the restrictions on individual preferences that might be required to generate consistent social orderings.

3 The Theory of Constitutions

It is at this point in my summary narrative that I should introduce my own origins of interest in public choice, and my own contributions, along with those of my colleague, Gordon Tullock. As did Duncan Black, I came to public choice out of intellectual frustration with orthodox pre-World War II public finance theory, at least as I learned it in the English language works of such economists as A. C. Pigou and Hugh Dalton in the UK, and Harold Groves and Henry Simons in the US. It made no sense to me to analyse taxes and public outlays independently of some consideration of the political process through which decisions on these two sides of the fiscal account were made. *Public finance theory could not be wholly divorced from a theory of politics.*

In coming to this basic criticism of the orthodoxy, I was greatly influenced by Wicksell on the one hand and by some of the Italian theorists on the other. One of my first published papers,[2] in 1949, was basically a plea for a better methodology. My initial reaction to Arrow's impossibility theorem was one of unsurprise. Since political outcomes emerge from a process in which many persons participate rather than from some mysterious group mind, why should anyone have ever expected 'social welfare functions' to be internally consistent? Indeed, as I argued in my 1954 paper on Arrow,[3] it seemed to me that, if individual preferences are such as to generate a cycle, then such a cycle, or such inconsistency, is to be preferred to consistency, since the latter would amount to the imposition of the will of some members of the group on others.

'Positive public choice'

The next stage in my logical sequence came when Gordon Tullock and I started to analyse how majority rules actually work – what Dennis Mueller has called 'positive public choice'. Tullock developed his now-classic 1959 paper on majority voting and log-rolling in which he showed that a sequence of majority votes on spending projects financed out of general tax revenues could over-extend the budget and could, indeed, make everyone worse off than they would be with no collective action.[4] Tullock's example was spending on many separate road projects all of which are financed from the proceeds of a general tax, but the same logic can be extended to any situation where there are several spending constituencies that independently influence budgetary patterns. We came to the view that the apparent ideological dominance of majority rule should be more thoroughly examined. This in turn required us to analyse alternatives to majority rule, and to begin to construct an 'economic theory of political constitutions', out of which came *The Calculus of Consent* in 1962. This book has achieved a measure of success, of course to our great satisfaction. We used ordinary economic assumptions about the utility-maximising behaviour of individuals, and we sought to explain why specific rules for making collective decisions might emerge from the constitutional level of deliberation.

To pull off this explanation, we needed some means or device that would enable us to pass from individually identifiable self-interest to something that might take the place of 'public interest'. Unless we could locate such a device or construct, we would have remained in the zero-sum model of politics, where any gains must be matched by losses. We got over this problem by looking at how rules for ordinary parlour games are settled *before* the fall of the cards is known. Uncertainty about just where one's own interest will lie in a sequence of plays or rounds of play will lead a rational person, from his own interest, to prefer rules or arrangements or constitutions that will seem to be 'fair', no matter what final positions he might occupy. You will, of course, recognise the affinity between this approach that Tullock and I used in *The Calculus of Consent* and that developed in much more general terms by John Rawls in his monumental treatise, *A Theory of Justice* (1971). Rawls had discussed his central notion of 'justice as fairness' in several papers published in the 1950s, and, while our approach came, we think, independently out of our own initial attempt to look for criteria for preferred rules, we do not quibble about the source of ideas. Indeed, the basic ideas in the 'justice as fairness' notion can also be found in the work of other scholars that predate Rawls's early papers.

Our book was a mixture of positive analysis of alternative decision rules and a normative defence of certain American political institutions that owe their origins to the Founding Fathers, and to James Madison in particular. We considered that our analysis did 'explain' features of the American political heritage that orthodox political science seemed unable to do. Explicitly and deliberately, we defended constitutional limits on majority voting. In a somewhat more fundamental sense, we defended the existence of constitutional constraints *per se*; we justified bounds on the exercise of majoritarian democracy. In this respect, I would argue that America's political history has been 'superior' to that of Britain, where neither in theory nor in practice have you imposed constraints on the exercise of parliamentary or legislative majorities comparable to those in America. For example, it would be difficult to conceive of an American cycle of nationalisation, denationalisation, and renationalisation of a basic industry merely upon shifts in the legislative majority between parties.

4 The Supply of Public Goods

I now want to get some of the early public choice contributions into methodological perspective. Black's early work on committees, Arrow's search for a social welfare function, our own work on the economic theory of constitutions, the derivations of these works in such applications as median voter models – all of these efforts were what we should now call *demand*-driven. By this I mean that the focus of attention was on the ways in which individual preferences might be amalgamated to generate collective results on the presumption that the outcomes would be there for the taking. There was almost no attention paid in these works to the utility-maximising behaviour of those who might be called on to *supply* the public goods and services demanded by the taxpayers-voters. There was no theory of public goods supply in the early models of public choice that I have discussed to this point.

Origins of public goods supply analysis

To get at the origins of the supply-side models, we must go back to some of the Italian scholars, who quite explicitly developed models of workings of the state-as-monopoly, analysed as being separate and apart from the citizenry, and with its own distinct interests. Machiavelli is, of course, the classic source of ideas here, but the discussions of Vilfredo Pareto and Gaetano Mosca about ruling classes, along with the fiscal applications by the public-finance theorists such as Antonio De Viti De Marco, Amilcare Puviani, and Mauro Fasiani all deserve mention in any catalogue.

From these writers, and independently of them, we may trace the development of rudimentary ideas through Joseph Schumpeter and then to Anthony Downs, who, in his 1957 book, *An Economic Theory of Democracy*, analysed political parties as analogous to profit-maximising firms. Parties, said Downs, set out to maximise votes, and he tried to explain aspects of observed political reality in terms of his vote-maximising models. Perhaps the most important theorem to emerge here was the tendency of parties to establish positions near each other in two-party competition and near the centre of the ideological or issue spectrum. William Riker (of the University of Rochester), in a significant 1962 book, challenged Downs's vote-maximising assumption, and argued convincingly that parties seek not maximum votes but only sufficient votes to ensure minimally winning coalitions.

Downs's primary emphasis was on the political party, not on the behaviour of the politician or bureaucrat. This gap in early supply-side analysis was filled by Gordon Tullock who, drawing on his own experiences in the bureaucracy of the US Department of State, published his *The Politics of Bureaucracy* in 1965, although he had written the bulk of this work a decade earlier. Tullock challenged the dominant orthodoxy of modern political science and public administration, exemplified in the works of Max Weber and Woodrow Wilson, by asking the simple question: What are the rewards and penalties facing a bureaucrat located in a hierarchy and what sorts of behaviour would describe his efforts to maximise his own utility? The analysis of bureaucracy fell readily into place once this question was raised. The mythology of the faceless bureaucrat following orders from above, executing but not making policy choices, and motivated only to forward the 'public interest', was not able to survive the logical onslaught. Bureaucrats could no longer be conceived as 'economic eunuchs'. It became obligatory for analysts to look at bureaucratic structure and at individual behaviour within that structure. Tullock's work was followed by a second Downs book, and the modern theory of bureaucracy was born.

Property rights and bureaucratic behaviour

As the theory of constitutions has an affinity with the work of Rawls, so the theory of bureaucracy has an affinity with the work of those economists who have been called the 'property rights theorists', such as Armen Alchian and Harold Demsetz of UCLA, and Roland McKean of Virginia, who initiated analysis of the influence of reward and punishment structures on individual behaviour, and especially in comparisons between profit and non-profit institutions. To predict behaviour, either in governmental bureaucracy or in privately organised non-proprietary institutions, it is necessary to examine carefully the constraints and opportunities faced by individual decision-makers.

The next step was almost as if programmed. Once we begin to look at bureaucracy in this way, we can, of course, predict that individual bureaucrats will seek to expand the size of their bureaus since, almost universally in modern Western societies, the salaries and perquisites of office are related directly to the sizes of budgets administered and controlled. The built-in motive force for expansion, the dynamics of modern governmental bureaucracy in the small and in the large, was apparent to all who cared to think. This theory of bureaucratic growth was formalised by William Niskanen, who developed a model of separate budget-maximising departments and sub-departments. In the limiting case, Niskanen's model suggested that bureaucracies could succeed in expanding budgets to twice the size necessary to meet taxpayers' genuine demands for public goods and services. In this limit, taxpayers end up by being no better off than they would be without any public goods; all of their net benefits are 'squeezed out' by the bureaucrats. The implication is that each and every public good or service, whether it be health services, education, transport, or defence, tends to be expanded well beyond any tolerable level of efficiency, as defined by the demands of the citizenry.

Alongside this theory of bureaucracy, there have been efforts to analyse the behaviour of the politicians, the elected legislators, who seek opportunities to earn 'political income'. Attempts have also been made (by Albert Breton and Randall Bartlett) to integrate demand-side and supply-side theories into a coherent analysis.

5 Rent-seeking

To this point, I have largely discussed what we might call established ideas in public choice, although this epithet should not imply that fascinating research is not continuing in some of the areas mentioned. But let me now briefly introduce an area of inquiry, 'rent-seeking', that is on the verge of blossoming. You may, if you prefer, call this 'profit-seeking', which might be descriptively more accurate. But 'rent-seeking' is used here in order to distinguish the activity from profit-seeking of the kind we ordinarily examine in our study of markets.

Once again, we can look to Gordon Tullock for the original work on rent-seeking, although he did not originally use that term, and did not, I think, fully appreciate the potential promised in his 1967 paper.[5]

Tullock's work has been followed by papers by Richard Posner, of the University of Chicago Law School, Anne Kreuger, of the University of Minnesota, who invented the term itself, and others, but my own prediction is that the genuine flurry of research activity in rent-seeking will occur only during the next decade.

What is 'rent-seeking'?

The basic notion is a very simple one and once again it represents the extension of standard price theory to politics. From price theory we learn that profits tend to be equalised by the flow of investments among prospects. The existence or emergence of an opportunity for differentially high profits will attract investment until returns are equalised with those generally available in the economy. What should we predict, therefore, when politics creates profit opportunities or rents? Investment will be attracted toward the prospects that seem favourable and, if 'output' cannot expand as in the standard market adjustment, we should predict that investment will take the form of attempts to secure access to the scarcity rents. When the state licenses an occupation, when it assigns import or export quotas, when it allocates TV spectra, when it adopts land-use planning, when it employs functionaries at above-market wages and salaries, we can expect resource waste in investments to secure the favoured plums.

Demands for money rents are elastic. The state cannot readily 'give money away' even if it might desire to do so. The rent-seeking analysis can be applied to many activities of the modern state, including the making of money transfers to specified classes of recipients. If mothers with dependent children are granted payments for being mothers, we can predict that we shall soon have more such mothers. If the unemployed are offered higher payments, we predict that the number of unemployed will increase. Or, if access to membership in recipient classes is arbitrarily restricted, we predict that there will be wasteful investment in rent-seeking. As the expansion of modern government offers more opportunities for rents, we must expect that the utility-maximising behaviour of individuals will lead them to waste more and more resources in trying to secure the 'rents' or 'profits' promised by government.

6 Empirical Public Choice

So much for a survey and narrative of the development of ideas in public-choice theory. I have to this point said little about the empirical testing of these ideas or hypotheses. In the last decade, these empirical tests have occupied much of the attention of public-choice economists. Indeed, to the Chicago-based group of scholars who talk about the 'economic theory of politics', the ideas that I have traced out above amount to little or nothing until they are tested; their view is that empirical work is the be-all and the end-all of the discipline. Those of us in the Virginia tradition are more catholic in our methodology; we acknowledge the contributions of the empiricists while attributing importance to the continuing search for new theoretical insights. The empiricists, among whom I should list my own colleagues Mark Crain and Bob Tollison, in addition to the Chicago group, notably George Stigler and Sam Peltzman, have taken the utility-maximising postulates and derived implications that are subject to test.

The Chicago-based emphasis has been on economic regulation of such industries as transport, broadcasting, and electricity. What is the economic model for the behaviour of the regulator and, through this, for the activities of the regulatory agency? What does the record show? Stigler suggested that the evidence corroborates the hypothesis that regulation is pursued in the interests of the industries that are regulated. Others have challenged Stigler and have tried to test the differing hypothesis that regulation is carried out for the self-interest of the regulatory bureaucracy, which may or may not coincide with the interest of the industry regulated. Little or none of the empirical work on regulation suggests that the pre-public-choice hypothesis of regulation in the 'public interest' is corroborated. In the long run, this research must have some impact on the willingness of the citizenry, and the politicians, to subject more and more of the economy to state regulation, although the end does not seem yet in sight.

Crain and Tollison have looked carefully at the record for legislatures in the American states. They have used straightforward utility-maximising models, with objectively measurable 'arguments' in the utility functions, to explain such things as relative salaries of legislators among states, relative occupational categories of legislators, committee structures in legislatures, varying lengths of legislative sessions. They have developed strong empirical support for the basic hypothesis that politicians respond to economic incentives much like the rest of us.

Political business cycles

A different area of empirical work that can be brought within the public-choice framework is that on 'political business cycles', i.e. the alleged attempt by politicians in office to create economic conditions timed so as to further their own electoral prospects. The results seem to be somewhat mixed, and I shall not attempt to offer any judgements on this research here.

7 Normative Implications of Public Choice

As some of you know, my own interests have never been in the empirical tradition, as narrowly defined. I have been more interested in a different sort of research inquiry that follows more or less naturally from the integration of the demand-side and the supply-side analysis of governmental decision-making institutions.

As proofs of the logical inconsistencies in voting rules are acknowledged, as the costs of securing agreement among persons in groups with differing preferences are accounted for, the theory of rules, or of constitutions, emerges almost automatically on the agenda for research, as I have already noted. But my own efforts have been aimed at going beyond the analysis of *The Calculus of Consent*. I have tried to move cautiously but clearly in the direction of normative understanding and evaluation, to move beyond analysis of the way rules work to a consideration of what rules work *best*.

Constitutional failure: the Leviathan state

In the last five years or so, my interest has been in examining the bases for constitutional improvement, for constitutional change, for what I have called 'constitutional revolution'. My efforts have been motivated by the observation that the American constitutional structure is in disarray; the constraints that 'worked' for two centuries seem to have failed. The checks on government expansion no longer seem to exist. The Leviathan state is the reality of our time. I state this for the US with certainty; I doubt that many of you would disagree concerning the UK.

My book, *The Limits of Liberty* (1975), was devoted to a diagnosis of this constitutional failure, a step that I considered to be necessary before reform might be addressed. (In this context, I found Nevil Johnson's 1977 book, *In Search of the Constitution*, with reference to Britain, to be congenial.) My current research emerges as a natural follow-up to the diagnosis. A first project has been completed. With Richard Wagner as co-author, we published *Democracy in Deficit* in early 1977, the theme of which is restated and applied to Britain with John Burton in the IEA's Hobart Paper No. 78, *The Consequences of Mr Keynes* (published in April 1978). The book was an attempt to examine the political consequences of Mr Keynes, and the central theme was to the effect that an important element of the American fiscal constitution, namely the balanced-budget rule, had been destroyed by the political acceptance of Keynesianism. Economists blindly ignored the asymmetry in application of Keynesian policy precepts, an asymmetry that the most elementary public-choice theorist would have spotted. They naïvely presumed that politicians would create budget surpluses as willingly as they create deficits. They forgot the elementary rule that politicians enjoy spending and do not like to tax.

In *Democracy in Deficit*, Wagner and I called explicitly for the restoration of budget balance as a constitutional requirement. With Geoffrey Brennan, I am now engaged in an attempt to design a 'tax constitution'.[6] We are examining ways and means through which the revenue-grabbing proclivities of governments might be disciplined by constitutional constraints imposed on tax bases and rates.

Can government be constrained?

These efforts, on my part and others, suggest that we proceed from a belief that governments can be constrained. We refuse to accept the Hobbesian scenario in which there are no means to bridle the passions of the sovereign. Historical evidence from America's own two centuries suggests that governments can be controlled by constitutions.

In once sense, all of public choice or the economic theory of politics may be summarised as the 'discovery' or 're-discovery' that people should be treated as rational utility-maximisers in *all* of their behavioural capacities. This central insight, in all of its elaborations, does not lead to the conclusion that all collective action, all government action, is necessarily undesirable. It leads, instead, to the conclusion that, because people will tend to maximise their own utilities, institutions must be designed so that individual behaviour will further the interests of the group, small or large, local or national. The challenge to us is one of constructing, or re-constructing, a political order that will channel the self-serving behaviour of participants towards the common good in a manner that comes as close as possible to that described for us by Adam Smith with respect to the economic order.

8 The Wisdom of Centuries

I have described the economic theory of politics, or public choice, as a relatively young subdiscipline that has emerged to occupy the attention of scholars in the three decades since the end of World War II. If we look only at the intellectual developments of the 20th century, public choice is 'new', and it has, I think, made a major impact on the way that living persons view government and political process. The public philosophy of 1978 is very different from the public philosophy of 1948 or 1958. There is now much more scepticism about the capacity or the intention of government to satisfy the needs of citizens.

At the start of my remarks, I stated that the ideas of public choice have been relatively slow to catch on in the UK. That statement is, I think, accurate, but I should be remiss if I did not end on a somewhat different note. In one sense, public choice – the economic theory of politics – is not new at all. It represents rediscovery and elaboration of a part of the conventional wisdom of the 18th and the 19th centuries, and notably the conventional wisdom that informed classical political economy. Adam Smith, David Hume, and the American Founding Fathers would have considered the central principles of public-choice theory to be so elementary as scarcely to warrant attention. A mistrust of governmental processes, along with the implied necessity to impose severe constraints on the exercise of governmental authority, was part and parcel of the philosophical heritage they all shared. This set of attitudes extended at least through the middle years of the 19th century, after which they seem to have been suspended for at least a hundred years. Perhaps they are on the way to return.

I could scarcely do better in conclusion than to introduce a citation from J. S. Mill's *Considerations on Representative Government* (1861):

... the very principle of constitutional government requires it to be assumed, that political power will be abused to promote the particular purposes of the holder; not because it always is so, but because such is the natural tendency of things, to guard against which is the especial use of free institutions.[7]

How much have we forgotten? Can modern man recover the wisdom of the centuries? Let us not despair. A start has been made.

Notes

1   For a discussion of the political setting for Keynesian economics, see J. M. Buchanan, John Burton and R. E. Wagner, *The Consequences of Mr Keynes*, Hobart Paper 78, IEA, April 1978. An extended treatment with primary application to an American setting is in James M. Buchanan and Richard E. Wagner, *Democracy in Deficit*, Academic Press, New York, 1977.
2   This paper, along with several other early papers, including my essay on the Italian writers, is reprinted in my book, *Fiscal Theory and Political Economy*, University of North Carolina Press, Chapel Hill, 1960.
3   Also included in the book cited *ibid.*
4   Gordon Tullock, 'Problems of Majority Voting', *Journal of Political Economy*, 67, December 1959, pp. 571–9.
5   'The Welfare Costs of Tariffs, Monopolies, and Theft', *Western Economic Journal*, June 1967.
6   Buchanan and Brennan, *The Power to Tax: Analytical Foundations of a Fiscal Constitution*, Cambridge University Press, 1980.
7   J. S. Mill, *Considerations on Representative Government* (1861), in J. S. Mill, *Essays on Politics and Society*, Vol. II, University of Toronto Press, Toronto, 1977, p. 505

Bibliography

Arrow, K. 1970: *Social Choice and Individual Values*. New Haven: Yale University Press, 2nd edition.
Bartlett, R. 1973: *Economic Foundation of Political Power*. New York: Free Press.
Black, D. 1958: *The Theory of Committees and Elections*. Cambridge: Cambridge University Press.
Black, D. and Newing, R. A. 1951: *Committee Decisions with Complementary Valuation*. London: William Hodge.

Breton, A. 1974: *The Economic Theory of Representative Government*. Chicago: Aldine.

Buchanan, J. M. 1960: *Fiscal Theory and Political Economy*. Chapel Hill: University of North Carolina Press.

Buchanan, J. M. 1967: *Public Finance in Democratic Process*. Chapel Hill: University of North Carolina Press.

Buchanan, J. M. 1975: *The Limits of Liberty: Between Anarchy and Leviathan*. Chicago: University of Chicago Press.

Buchanan, J. M. 1978: *Freedom in Constitutional Contract*. College Station: Texas A & M University Press.

Buchanan, J. M. and Tullock, G. 1962: *The Calculus of Consent: Logical Foundations of Constitutional Democracy*. Ann Arbor: University of Michigan Press.

Buchanan, J. M. and Wagner, R. E. 1977: *Democracy in Deficit: the Political Legacy of Lord Keynes*. New York: Academic Press.

Buchanan, J. M. and Tollison, R. (eds) 1972: *Theory of Public Choice*. Ann Arbor: University of Michigan Press.

Downs, A. 1957: *An Economic Theory of Democracy*. New York: Harper.

Downs, A. 1967: *Inside Bureaucracy*. Boston: Little, Brown.

Niskanen, W. A. 1971: *Bureaucracy and Representative Government*. Chicago: Aldine.

Olson, M. 1965: *The Logic of Collective Action*. Cambridge, Mass: Harvard University Press.

Riker, W. 1962: *The Theory of Political Coalitions*. New Haven: Yale University Press.

Riker, W. and Ordeshook, P. 1973: *An Introduction to Positive Political Theory*. Englewood Cliffs, NJ: Prentice Hall.

Sen, A. K. 1970: *Collective Choice and Social Welfare*. San Francisco: Holden Day.

Tullock, G. 1965: *The Politics of Bureaucracy*. Washington DC: Public Affairs Press.

Tullock, G. 1970: *Private Wants, Public Means*. New York: Basic Books.

Tullock, G. 1972: *Towards a Mathematics of Politics*. Ann Arbor: University of Michigan Press.

Tullock, G. 1974: *The Social Dilemma*. Blacksburg: Center for Study of Public Choice.

Wicksell, K. 1896: *Finanztheoretische Untersuchungen*. Jena: Gustav Fischer. A major portion of this work is translated and published under the title 'A New Principle of Just Taxation', in R. A. Musgrave and A. T. Peacock (eds), 1959: *Classics in the Theory of Public Finance*. London: Macmillan.

Note: References above are limited to books. A listing of article-length contributions would extend to many pages. See the Bibliography in Dennis Mueller's survey paper in *Journal of Economic Literature* 14 (2), June 1976, pp. 395–433.

4

Monopoly in Money and Inflation

with H. Geoffrey Brennan

I Setting the Stage: the Politics of Money

1 The Little Alchemist: Two Versions of a Fable

Version A

Once upon a time, deep in the forest, there lived a little alchemist who spent all his time searching for a way to turn sand into gold. One dreary winter's day, his efforts were rewarded. He found a secret formula with which he could make all the gold he could ever want from the sand near his cottage.

The little alchemist could then make gold and exchange it for anything his heart desired. He first built a fine castle, and filled it with beautiful things. He hired many servants: maids, cooks, butlers, gardeners, and coachmen. His table was graced with gourmet foods from throughout the land. He equipped a stable with fine horses. The procession of pretty ladies who came to visit the castle suggested to some rather cynical observers that the little alchemist used his gold to purchase almost anything.

All the other people in the land were made poorer by the alchemist's discovery, since they gave up the goods and the labour that went into building the castle, training the fine horses, growing and eating the food, and even the pleasure of the fine ladies. Those others did not, of course, realise that the new gold made by the little alchemist simply reduced the

Published originally as Hobart Paper No. 88, IEA (1981).

exchange value of all the other gold in the land, which had been, for ages, used for money.

Version B

The little alchemist discovered the secret formula for turning sand into gold. But, before he made any gold, he decided to put on his economics thinking cap. He wanted to consider the effects of his discovery on all the people in the land. The little alchemist understood that he could, if desired, make gold and use it to buy all the good things he wanted. But he also understood that these things would have to come from somebody; others would have to give up the goods and labour to satisfy his desires. While he would become very rich, others in the land would become poorer. Since the little alchemist *cared about other people* as well as himself, he decided not to use his discovery at all. He did not make even so much as one ounce of gold from sand. He built no fine castle; he hired no servants. Instead, he destroyed the secret formula, never again to be found.

Alchemist not foolish: government foolish?

What would a girl of 10 say if we read our two versions of the fable to her? She would accept the first, but probably reject the second as totally 'untrue'. No little alchemist would be so foolish as to destroy his means of getting very rich.

Nonetheless, sophisticated thinkers are not supposed to have the wisdom of the 10-year-old, because the second version is precisely the sort of story we have all been supposed to believe for centuries whenever questions about the authority of governments to print money are raised. If we do nothing more than replace the words 'little alchemist' by 'government', and the word 'gold' by 'paper money' in the fable, the similarity becomes self-evident. Government possesses the power to create money and exchange it for goods and services, but we are supposed to believe it will use this power only in the 'public interest' and refrain from using it to purchase the things it may desire.

The fable of the little alchemist helps us to get a realistic perspective on government and inflation. If government has the power to create something without cost that will enable it to purchase things it wants, surely childlike wisdom would suggest that such power will be used.

Why has this self-evident proposition been so widely overlooked and misunderstood throughout the ages? Why have very intelligent men and women been led to accept the unrealistic version of the fable?

2 But 'Money is Different'

There are two parts of the answer to this question. The first would suggest that 'money is different' (below), the second that 'government is benevolent' (section 3, pp. 51–3).

Economists have emphasised that money is indeed different from ordinary goods and services. We do not have to master the intricacies of monetary theory to appreciate that money serves a quite different function from that of an ordinary commodity. We do not 'eat money' or 'wear it on our back'. Money is useful because it facilitates the operation of the whole economy. It has often been referred to as the 'grease' that makes the economic wheels go around.

Free competition in money may not guarantee efficiency

This difference in function does not, however, necessarily suggest that the competitive market economy, within a framework of law, would not or could not operate so that something would emerge as 'money' which would be supplied and demanded like other commodities and services. Even in the total absence of governmental action, money would emerge in some form. But economists have argued, with considerable persuasiveness, that money is different also in the sense that free competition may not guarantee efficiency.

Suppose there were a régime of 'free entry into money creation'. Anyone could set up a bank and begin to accept deposits, make loans, and issue bank notes. Such a régime might be highly vulnerable to waves of expansion and contraction.

The conjectural history of the goldsmith illustrates the argument. The goldsmith takes his clients' gold pieces for safe-keeping. Experience teaches him that only a small proportion of his clients will demand a return of their deposits on any particular day. Therefore, he commences to lend out a portion of these deposits, holding only a fraction of gold in reserve, designed to meet demands for return by depositors. In so doing, the goldsmith 'creates' new money. Both the old and new depositors treat the same gold as money for their purposes. But there may come a day when a disproportionately large number of depositors simultaneously demand a return of their initial deposits of gold pieces. The goldsmith cannot honour all claims. Evidence of this incapacity will, in turn, cause still other depositors to present their claims. There will be a 'run' on the bank which, spread throughout the economy, would mean financial crisis.

There seems to be nothing in the competitive-market structure to keep the supply of money in the economy from being expanded too rapidly in 'fair weather' and contracted too sharply in 'foul weather'. Because of the peculiarities of money, the competitive market will 'fail'. A governmental rôle in defining and/or regulating the value of the monetary unit seems to follow from the demonstration.

The minimally required governmental rôle may be limited to desig-nating a specific commodity, gold or silver, or some other commodity (or combination of commodities) as the money unit, along with a pledge to purchase and sell it for a fixed price. The forces of the competitive economy would, in this setting, continue to be relied on to generate supplies of the monetary commodity in line with demands at the fixed price or value. This essentially was the idealised model considered relevant during the 19th-century heyday of the international gold standard. Even then the system did not work as well as the simple model might have predicted, largely because of the fractional reserve basis for monetary expansion and contraction that remained (the amount of paper money permitted was a percentage of the gold reserves).

Governmental monetary function thought necessary because of inherent market 'instability'

In this century, a somewhat different argument has been used to support a much more active rôle for government in monetary matters. The competitive market economy may be inherently unstable, it is argued, even if we disregard the monetary sources of instability. In this basically Keynesian or post-Keynesian approach, a governmental responsibility for promoting stability in income and in employment seems to follow. And many governments were assigned this rôle after the Great Depression of the 1930s.

To meet this responsibility, it is said, government must have tools to influence aggregate demand or aggregate spending. Hence, government should be granted authority to issue and to destroy money. This money-issue power offers an effective means of increasing aggregate demand during periods of depression, either by direct government spending or by the distribution of cash, and of reducing aggregate demand during periods of inflation. A government without such powers might be severely handicapped in trying to fulfil its stabilisation rôle. (Note that this argument is used to justify much more than a governmental rôle in setting a *fixed* value on some designated monetary commodity.)

3   And 'Government is Benevolent'

The 'market failure' argument, in either one of the two forms noted, has been used to justify governmental intervention in the regulation of the economy's monetary affairs. The demonstration of market failure does not itself, however, justify a governmental rôle. To do so, it must be accompanied by analysis and demonstration of how government will act in carrying out the rôle assigned to it. In the absence of some view of how the political–governmental process works, 'market failure' provides no grounds for the delegation of money creation authority to government. This elementary methodological truth has been overlooked and/or neglected by far too many modern economists, political scientists, sociologists, and other social scientists. Almost without consideration, economists who have discussed questions of economic policy, including monetary institutions, have accepted implicitly what can only be called an unrealistic, naïve, unhistorical, Utopian, 'benevolent despot' image of government.

This 'benevolent despot' designation is convenient because economists have placed themselves in positions of proffering advice on policy reform, as if the political decision-makers, whoever these may be, will accept and act on such advice in total independence from any human motivations or impulses that political decision-makers themselves might possess. As a result of this somewhat bizarre stance, economists have made suggestions on policy proposals that totally ignore the working of politics, with the result that proposals finally adopted have often become perverted versions of the original suggestions.

Keynesian fiscal policy creates bias towards deficits

The most dramatic and the most important example is provided in the Keynesian theory of fiscal policy concerning the use of the government budget for national economic stabilisation. The Keynesian policy rule is simple: create budget deficits during periods when there is a shortfall in aggregate demand; create budget surpluses during periods when there is excessive aggregate demand. Such a policy rule, however, would only be implemented by a benevolent authoritarian political régime. In ordinary democracies, whether of the British parliamentary or the American Congressional variety, elected politicians and parties will gladly create deficits. They like to spend; they do not enjoy levying taxes on constituents. But they will rarely, if ever, deliberately create budget surpluses. They do not like to reduce spending or to increase taxes. Even slight attention to the relevance of normal political behaviour should have suggested that the Utopian Keynesian rule for fiscal policy would produce biases towards budget deficits.[1]

As early as 1896, the great Swedish economist, Knut Wicksell, warned his colleagues about the folly of assuming government to be a 'benevolent despot' in talking about matters of economic policy. He notes that such an assumption about government was likely to distract attention away from constructive reform, which must focus on prospects for changing the rules and institutions through which policy outcomes are generated from the interactions of political decision-makers who are fallible persons like the rest of us.

In the second version of our fable, the little alchemist tries to promote the general interest of the whole community. There can, in this version, be no argument for imposing restrictions on his behaviour. There may be a rôle for the economist, in this story, in pointing out the consequences of alternative actions, so that the benign little alchemist may be better informed on exactly what 'doing good' entails. More ambitiously, the social scientist *qua* moral philosopher may wish to assist the alchemist in defining what is 'good' in a more abstract sense. But there can be no argument here for restrictions on the alchemist's behaviour, for rules chosen in advance to guard against the worst possible outcomes: such restrictions can only inhibit him from carrying forward the 'public interest'.

Pervasiveness of the 'benevolent despot' image

This benevolent despot image of the political process has been pervasive in the policy attitudes of political economists. And it has naturally directed attention to the sorts of activities that make sense in the benevolent despot setting – tracing out the effects of alternative policy choices, and preaching the message of what effects are 'good'. But once we so much as admit the possibility that such an image of government may be unduly optimistic, we turn naturally to consider whether there may be prospects for reform in a different direction – by changing the political institutions, the rules that govern the behaviour of political decision-makers.

Constitutional requirements for budget balance, for tax and spending limits, for restricted rules on money issue make little sense if government is assumed always to do good on its own account. It is on this basis that many accomplished, if politically naïve, economists have actively opposed such proposals. The benevolent despot image of government has simply blinded them to the need to guard against dangers that should seem real and obvious enough once they are pointed out – even to a 10-year-old!

4 Democratic Electoral Constraints on Government

Our argument that government should not be explicitly or implicitly conceived in the 'benevolent despot' image may be readily accepted. But our fable of the little alchemist may still be thought inappropriate as an analogue to governmental powers of money creation. While it may be conceded that government will not act like the little alchemist in the second version of our fable, the argument may still be made that neither will government act selfishly like our hero in the first version.

Government, it will be suggested, is not able to do as 'it' pleases. There is no 'it'. There is no monolithic entity that 'behaves' analogously to a single person. Government is a very complex interaction process in which politicians and officials participate in varying rôles. The outcomes of governmental action may not reflect the motivations of any single actor. In democratic societies, government is constrained explicitly by the voters. If those who govern on behalf of the voters should try to act contrary to the general 'public interest', or at the least as this interest might be interpreted by a majority of the voters in the electorate, they will be disciplined through the electoral process. Politicians who act contrary to voters' desires will be replaced in political office by others who will follow voters' desires more closely.

'Public-choice' analysis shows weakness of democratic restraints on government

This idealised model for the operation of democratic electoral constraints on the independent powers of government has come under increasing critical scrutiny, and especially so from the research developments in 'public choice' that have emerged during the decades after World War II. Periodic elections may prove relatively ineffective in restricting the discretionary powers of agents who act for the public in decision-making rôles. Bureaucrats may be able to set the agenda for legislative actions, and the motivations of elected legislators may coincide more closely with those of the bureaucracy than with those of the voting constituency. Organised group interests may be able to use the fiscal and regulatory powers of government to promote results that explicitly run counter to the general interests of all voters.

The observed rates of growth of governments, in most Western nations since World War II, make it increasingly difficult to support any 'demo-cratically constrained' model of politics. Relatively few modern observers are willing to attribute the observed increases in total government fiscal and regulatory activity exclusively to the ultimate demands of voters for increased quantities of governmentally financed goods and services. Observers have come increasingly to acknowledge that governments have some internal dynamic of their own, that they act, and grow, largely independently of the wishes of the citizenry. The 19th- and early 20th-century faith in the efficacy of electoral controls over politicians seems to have been ill-placed; and the differences, on balance, between nominally democratic régimes – as in the USA, UK, etc. – and nominally non-democratic régimes – as in the Latin American military dictatorships – seem considerably less relevant, at least for monetary and budgetary policy, than they might at one time have appeared.

5 Government as Monopolist

We propose to analyse government in a manner directly analogous to our first version of the fable of the self-seeking little alchemist. We shall abstract completely from democratic electoral constraints of the standard variety. Voters are taken to have no effective control over governmental policy, whether on money issue or anything else, through the ordinary electoral processes. Politicians and political parties may rotate in elected office, but such rotation does not really modify the central thrust of self-seeking governmental actions.

We need not assume that all political agents all of the time act in some narrowly defined self-interest and contrary to their versions of the 'public interest'. Our analysis is justified even if public-spirited behaviour is widespread on the part of politicians and bureaucrats. All we need do is to allow that there may be politicians and bureaucrats who, at least on occasion, will act in accordance with what we might call their 'natural proclivities', and that these run counter to the basic desires of the citizenry. If only this much be accepted, we are warranted in trying to analyse government behaviour in the 'worst-case' setting where such natural proclivities predominate.

In a sense, our analysis is similar to that which has dominated economic-policy discussion and which was criticised above. Our supposition of 'malevolent despotism' is designed for a purpose: to offer a setting within which we can begin to discuss constructive reform in the external constraints on the exercise of governmental powers to create money, to tax, or to regulate the economy.

Clearly, there would be little or no purpose in examining the behaviour of any 'worst-case' government, if we accepted as prejudgement the notion that no external limits could possibly be effective in constraining the powers and authority granted. Given such a prejudgement, the best we might do would be to join the 'preachers' who try to convince politicians or officials that they should act 'morally'. Our whole approach, in this *Hobart Paper* and in earlier writings, is based on the presupposition that *constitutional constraints* on governmental behaviour can be effective, even if direct electoral controls are not.[2]

We assume the possible enforceability of constitutional checks and limits. Some analysis of the way that governments might be expected to behave under an explicit grant of money-issue power is then warranted. Quite apart from predictions on how governments might, in some average sense, use this power, to us it seems methodologically naïve to presume that governments, reflected in the actions of their agents, will behave benevolently rather than in accordance with their natural proclivities. Indeed, even as a predictive technique, 'natural government' seems superior to 'benevolent government'. This superiority is suggested by nothing more than a casual glance at the historical record, which clearly indicates that governments throughout the ages have tended to abuse the money-creation authority granted to them. Examples abound: Germany in the 1920s, Hungary in 1945–46, Britain in 1972–73, the United States in 1978–79, ...

We shall use the term *monopoly government* to distinguish our basic conception from both *benevolent government*, which has dominated orthodox economic policy discussion, and *electorally constrained government*, which has been reflected in 'public-choice' literature.

Economic theory of monopoly applied to governmental monetary behaviour

We take the term 'monopoly' directly from economic theory, and much of the discussion involves rather straightforward application of the theory of monopoly in industry [part II of this chapter]. Standard monopoly theory may be usefully compared with our extension to government. In economics, the monopolist is supposed always to exploit fully the profit potential of his entitlement or opportunity. Is this strictly how the individual monopolist behaves? Clearly not, since we may reckon that some monopolists may take into account the interests of potential customers, as well as much else. A monopolist may not choose to exploit fully the potential profit opportunity that his market power grants him. He may not behave strictly as wealth-maximising *Homo economicus*, for any number of reasons: he may, for example, prefer the 'quiet life'.

Nonetheless, the theory of how the monopoly firm works is highly useful. It is properly conceived as an 'as if' theory that enables us to analyse conceptually the 'worst-case', to indicate the natural limits of consumers' vulnerability to exploitation, to define the maximal distortions in resource usage that monopoly can generate. And, on the basis of this theory, we can discuss the ways and means through which monopoly positions may be avoided and through which, if attained, they may be made short-lived.

The extension of this monopoly analysis to the government's use of its power to create money may be defended methodologically on precisely similar grounds. The theory of monopoly government, based on the notion that the monopoly powers will be exploited to the maximum, becomes a necessary ingredient to any constructive discussion of possible constitutional constraints. The theory need not be taken to imply that governments will always, or even on average, act as maximising monopolists. It does, nonetheless, allow us to set the limits to potential exploitation of the inherent or natural monopoly granted to government in money creation.

Specifically, we postulate that, if granted an unrestricted monopoly franchise to issue money, government will maximise the 'revenues' it can secure from this authority.[3] More correctly, and especially since the use of this power will cause inflation, the monopoly government will maximise its *real* revenues, its command over goods and services, the *real* value of the purchases it may make in the economy. In this setting, consider once again the first version of our fable of the little alchemist, which may now be extended to make the central point in this whole *Paper*. There will be natural limits on the amount of new gold he will want to make from sand, even if there is little or no cost. These limits will be set at the maximum value of real goods and services he can purchase with new gold.

By analysing government as a monolithic maximising entity, we are not, of course, suggesting that each and every person who participates in the very complex interaction of governmental decision processes devotes his or her energies solely to maximising real revenue for the government as a whole. Government, of course, is not a single entity. Our positive model is an abstract formulation that allows us to cut through the complexities of differential personal motivation and impose the unique 'maximand' as the objective. Again, some comparison with the orthodox theory of the monopoly firm becomes relevant. A firm also makes decisions with the involved participation of many persons, who might have quite different personal motivations. But economists apparently find it illuminating to treat profits as the unique maximand. Our use of real revenues as the maximand for monopoly government is essentially identical.

Much of the following analysis, developed in some detail in part II of this chapter, is elementary. The critical threshold to be surmounted is the acceptance of the relevance and usefulness of the notion of monopoly in government behaviour. Once this threshold is crossed, the first version of our fable indicates that the central problem in inflation is the monopoly wielded by government in creating money.

II Analysis: Unrestrained Government Monopoly in Creating Money

6 Monopoly Franchises in Money Creation

The *status quo* provides ample empirical evidence that our whole exercise is grounded in reality. Most national governments in 1981 possess monopoly franchises in the creation of money, in one form or another. To our knowledge, no country allows a totally free market in money, and none limits the governmental rôle to the definition of value of a monetary unit in support of a pure commodity standard. Departures from strict monopoly franchises exist for a few small countries that tie their own currency values to that of larger currencies. Almost universally, national governments hold the authority to issue paper or fiat currency, either directly through governmental treasuries (as in Great Britain) or indirectly through governmentally controlled central banks (as in Switzerland).

International influences on domestic money monopolist

National governments do not, of course, exist in total isolation, one from another, and the relationships among the separate national economies necessarily exert 'feedback' constraints on the domestic money-creation power. Most fundamentally, to the extent that citizens and corporations within a single country find it possible to hold balances, transact business, and make contracts designated in monies of other nations, the monopoly position of the home country government is weakened.

A truly international economy, in which citizens of all countries could deal in any one of many competing national monies, might seem to offer one means of substantially eliminating the monopoly power of any single national government.[4] But this 'solution' seems highly vulnerable as soon as we ask the simple question: Why would we expect any national government, now in possession of a money-creation monopoly franchise, to allow its citizens to make domestic transactions (including paying taxes) in the monies of other governments? Why would we expect any monopolist to allow its own profit opportunity to be eroded when it can exercise legal authority to prevent it? So long as national governments hold the legal power to define what shall be money for purposes of paying taxes, incurring debt obligations and making contracts, we must surely expect that this power will be used rather than abandoned. And this straightforward prediction is indirectly supported by the arguments of economists against competitive markets in money issue discussed in part I.

In the analysis of part II, we shall neglect the rôle that competitive constraints arising from the international economy might play in affecting the exploitation of the monopoly franchise in money. We do not, of course, deny that such constraints exist or that they are always insignificant. Even for a very large economy, the exchange value of its national currency relative to that issued by other countries will exert feedback influences on the issuing agent, even if we model the behaviour of this authority strictly in revenue-maximising terms. As in several other aspects of our analysis, however, we abstract from this feature. It seems prudent to put first things first. We shall model money-issue as if government is assigned a monopoly franchise in a *closed economy*. We leave it to others to modify the basic analysis as required to extend it as appropriate to an open economy.

7 Transactions Value of Money in a Non-inflationary Economy

Money performs a function of real value. It is not merely a veil. Persons will voluntarily exchange real goods and services for money units, even if they have no intrinsic worth and cannot be directly consumed or utilised. Money is valued for its instrumental usage in facilitating future exchanges. So long as people expect government either to accept money in payment of taxes or to give back real goods and services for money at a future date, government will be able to 'sell' pieces of paper designated 'money'. The real value of the money issue will be the *transactions* value that money serves in the economy.

Real capital value of monopolistic money issue

The government monopolist in money issue can secure this value even in a régime that is totally non-inflationary. Suppose society shifts abruptly from a pure barter to a money economy. The government simply issues a given nominal stock of money, M, as pieces of paper that will be used as media of exchange. Because of its value for transactions, individuals will 'purchase' this paper with goods and services, which the government will then have for its own use.

   How much value in goods and services will people 'pay' for this money issue? What do they give up in each period in order to hold M units of money? – presumably real assets that could earn a rate of return, r, per period. The discounted value of the pieces of paper in the quantity, M, will, therefore, be $r.M/r$ or, simply, M. This real capital value of the money issue is independent of the quantity of nominal money issued by government. The same real value can be secured whether 1,000, 1,000,000, or 1,000,000,000 units (pieces of paper) are printed, because the quantity issued will determine the level of prices for goods and services. And larger quantities of nominal units will have to be deflated by precisely corresponding larger price indices in order to compute the real value of the total issue. To say that the government captures real value, M, from its money issue we must therefore specify that M is designated in prices that will be set initially and which will prevail permanently since no additional money is to be issued.[5]

   In this extremely rarified setting (the assumed non-inflationary régime), the government has no problem of making a choice. The government cannot issue more money in periods after the first, and, more importantly, people who 'purchase' the pieces of paper act as if they think there will be no government issue in later periods. In this setting, and under the assumed non-inflationary constraint, government is securing revenue from its monopoly power, but there is no maximising calculus. It will secure the full transactions value of money from *any* amount of issue.

Possible behaviour of a 'do-gooding' government money monopolist

If the monopoly monetary authority should, out of some motivation to 'do good', decide that it has no need or desire for the real revenue stemming from its franchise in money, it would have to do something to avoid making profits from its creation of money. It could proceed in either of two ways. It could pay all holders of money a rate of return, r, on their holdings, that it could presumably finance by general taxes on the citizenry. Or, alternatively, the government could define its pieces of paper so that the nominal number of units shrinks by the proportion r in each period, producing gradual deflation.

Under either procedure, the real capital value of the initial issue could be reduced to zero. In the first case, the holders of money receive the full transactions value of money in the economy, and without payment. The second procedure might possibly be arranged so that the holders of the nominal units of money would, in a sense, pay the taxes to subsidise themselves, which suggests that on equity grounds the second of the two methods might be preferred.[6]

8 Real Revenue Potential in Excess of Transactions Value

Despite its usefulness in setting our analysis, we cannot simply *assume* a non-inflationary régime. And, as the discussion of the monopoly firm suggested (pp. 56–7), we do not propose to proceed as if governmental benevolence will produce non-inflationary monetary régimes. The preceding analysis was designed only to emphasise that real revenues may accrue from the possession of the money-creation franchise, even in the total absence of inflation. It was not intended to suggest that such a régime would emerge.

Such a prediction, given our concept of government as a maximiser of real revenue, could be made only if it could somehow demonstrate that the transactions value of money is also the maximum value that the government could exact from the full exploitation of the monopoly money franchise. Such a proposition will not, in general, be valid, and the non-inflationary scenario would be approximated only under a very restrictive set of circumstances (pp. 59–60).

Full transactions value of money

In the non-inflationary régime, the holder of the franchise could secure the full transactions value of money in the economy independently of the quantity of nominal issue (pp. 59–60).[7] If individuals expect that the size of the initial-period issue will remain permanently fixed, and that no further money creation will take place, and if they act on these expectations, the level of prices in the economy will adjust itself in direct proportion to the size of the nominal issue in the initial period. This relationship has often been stated in terms of the elasticity of demand for nominal money units, which remains at unity in the setting postulated; that is, a percentage increase in supply produces an exactly equal percentage decrease in demand.

In such a model the costs of holding a unit of money or cash is simply the rate of return that could be secured on an income-earning asset that could be purchased with that unit. For a single period, and setting the size of the unit at one, this cost is simply r.

How might the monopoly holder of the money-creation franchise extract more than the pure transactions value of money from citizens? It may do so by increasing the costs of holding cash balances above r, that is, by reducing the value of previously-issued nominal units of money by issuing new money in subsequent periods.

Suppose a person chooses to hold £1 in cash for one period when r is 10 per cent. The cost is 10 pence. He (or she) expects the £1 to possess the *same* capital value, by which we mean the same purchasing power over goods and services, at the end of the period as it had at the beginning. Suppose, however, that, during the period the initial-period money issue, M, is doubled, and the holder of the £1 finds that prices have doubled. At the end of the period, the £1 will purchase only one-half the quantity of goods and services it could command at the start. The cost of holding the cash balance turns out to be 60 pence, as compared to 10 pence under the non-inflationary régime.

As this simple example suggests, the monopolist secures the pure transactions value of money in the economy, M, immediately on the initial issue. But more real value can be gained from the franchise by reducing the 'capital value' that persons have placed on money balances at the time they made decisions to hold cash. In the example, the 'capital value' of the £1 is reduced by one-half.

The limits to the monetary monopolist's real revenue

In the limit, the real revenue that the monopolist might gain may be much beyond that indicated in this example, given the state of expectations implicit in the analysis to this point. By issuing a sufficiently large quantity of nominal money in the second period, after people have made their decisions about holding cash balances based on the initial-period issue, the monopolist can reduce the capital values on the existing nominal units of money almost to zero.

Suppose that nominal units in the amount M are issued initially; people think this will be the fixed and permanent amount of nominal money in the economy and make plans accordingly. Suppose, now, the monetary authority issues 1,000 M in the second period. The holders of the initial M units of money will find the pieces of paper worth only 1/1,000 of what they expected when they made their initial decisions to hold cash.

The sequence may continue. Suppose that, with the 1,001 M in existence in the second period, people expect no subsequent money creation. They make plans to hold cash as before, but now a third period comes along and the monetary authority issues still more money in the amount of 1,000,000 M. In the limit, the monopolist may, at a maximum under this set of circumstances, secure the transactions value of money in the economy *in each and every period of time*, instead of only once, as in the non-inflationary régime. The monopolist is able to do this because he succeeds in wiping out the capital value of all previously existing money at the onset of each period. To the individual the cost of holding £1 in cash for a single period approaches £1.10.[8]

9 But the People Cannot be Fooled all the Time

This 'scenario' neglects an important constraint that will emerge to prevent such extreme exploitation of the monopolist's position. It is relevant only in the setting where all who make decisions to hold money balances do so in the continuing expectation that no additional money will be issued. In other words, people continue to hold the *same real value* of cash despite the continuing confiscation of the capital values of the cash they have held.

It is, of course, unrealistic to attribute such behaviour to all persons. The 'scenario' is, nonetheless, highly useful since it sets the extreme *upper limit* to the real revenue that a money-creation monopolist can gain from such a franchise. And so long as *anyone* acts in this way the gains to the government money-monopolist will include not only the transactions value of money but also the confiscations of the capital values in the cash held.

Analytical usefulness of assumption of individual rationality

But what if *all* individuals form their expectations 'rationally'? Modern-day economists are likely to shift all too readily to suppose that behaviour is at the opposite extreme from that argued here. They are likely to attribute rationality to everyone, as though all individuals act like highly trained economists. Nonetheless, working out the analysis under such extreme rationality assumptions is also useful for our purposes, because it should provide us with a lower limit to the present value of the money-creation franchise.

Suppose, now, that each person knows he (or she) confronts a revenue-maximising government monopolist of money issue. What sort of behaviour will be attributed to the monopolist? And how will decisions about holding cash be affected by such predictions about the monopolist's behaviour?

First, given any expectation of new money issues, a *lower real value* of wealth will be held in cash than otherwise. That is, the higher the costs of holding cash in real terms, the less will be held.

Second, and more complex, if the individual expects that the capital value of *any* cash balance he or she chooses to hold will be totally confiscated, or almost so, by inflationary issue of new currency, will it be rational to hold any balances at all? It seems likely that very few, and possibly none, of the individuals would hold money balances where they fully anticipated that their capital values would be almost totally wiped out by inflation. Ultimately, the economy would return to a barter régime. And although the monopolist holds the franchise to create money, none will then be accepted by citizens. The government will be unable to purchase goods and services with its pieces of paper labelled *Money*. The value of the monopoly franchise becomes zero.

10 The Credibility Dilemma

A dilemma thus exists if citizens are fully 'rational'. Individuals, as potential holders and users of money, find themselves unable to enjoy the genuine resource-saving economies that monetary transactions represent because of the anticipated prohibitive cost of holding cash. The resort to barter is grossly inefficient, but less so for the prospective holder than the anticipated confiscation of the capital value of balances. These potential holders and users of money would be willing to give up real goods for the services of money if, in some way, they could be insured against such confiscation.

At the same time, the governmental monopolist holding the money-creation franchise finds itself unable to exploit the potential profit that seems to exist. Since money creation, as such, is essentially costless, it would, of course, like to be able to purchase real goods and services with the pieces of paper, but it is prevented from so doing because people are unwilling to accept them.

Unexploited 'gains-from-trade'

There are unexploited 'gains-from-trade' as between the potential holders/users of money and the monetary authority. But, also, the agreement that might guarantee net benefits to both parties may be very difficult to negotiate due to the absence of effective enforcing mechanisms. There may be no means of negotiating a contract that both parties consider binding.

The monetary authority may seek to resolve the apparent *impasse* here by pre-announcement. It may announce a specific time-sequence for the issue of money over a whole set of periods. (Section 12 analyses the choice calculus of the monetary monopolist in selecting such a path of issue in the expectation that it will be binding and that people so consider it.) But will individuals *believe* the pre-announcement and make their balance-holding plans accordingly? Will it be rational for them to do so?

Suppose the government issues M units of nominal money and announces that no more money will be issued. (This example could readily be modified to allow for any specific pre-announced rate of issue.) Suppose that everyone accepts the announcement in the belief that government is honest. They then shift the preferred share of their wealth into cash. It is evident that this capital value is ready for the taking by government should it choose to renege on its promise. By inflating the money issue beyond its commitment, government can confiscate almost the full capital value of any money balances previously accumulated. In so doing, of course, it will lose its credibility. People might believe such an announcement at one time, but having seen their capital confiscated through inflation subsequently, they are unlikely to be fooled again. Under what conditions will it be rational for the potential holder and user of money to anticipate that the government will renege?

11 The Discount Rate for Government

If the government recognises in advance that it will lose credibility by reneging on its promise concerning future money issue, will it refrain from breaking such a promise? The answer clearly depends on the discount rate that describes the monopolist's behaviour.

Suppose the monopolist issues a quantity of nominal money initially, and promises that it will never issue additional quantities. If people believe the promise, government can secure the full present value of the money in the initial period, which it may either consume or invest in income-earning assets. If it invests in income-earning assets, the monopolist can collect an income in each period. But, in any subsequent period, it can, by a once-and-for-all inflation of issue (after which it may be able to secure no acceptance of new money), get approximately the full transactions value once again. If the discount rate is higher than the rate of return on investment, it seems evident that the rational government will renege on its commitment. If its discount rate is below the rate of return on investment, the government, even if it continues to act as a strict net revenue-maximiser, will rationally keep its word.

The monetary monopolist's rate of discount seems to depend on the ability to make portfolio adjustments, and on the anticipated permanence of the franchise.

Portfolio adjustment

For an individual, we do not ask what his private rate of discount is because we assume that he faces a market-determined rate to which portfolios are adjusted. Hence, at the appropriate margin of decision, the individual is always discounting at the market rate. It follows that he remains on the margin of indifference between continuing to hold a particular asset and cashing it in at market value and either consuming or re-investing the proceeds in alternative earning opportunities (transactions costs ignored). In application to the problem of choice that faces the monetary monopolist, the discount rate to which it adjusts itself would, indeed, be the market rate if it is able to adjust its portfolio like that of a private investor, and if its impact on the relevant market is small.

Since we are examining the behaviour of government as the holder of the money-creation franchise, it may seem far-fetched to discuss its portfolio adjustment as if it were a utility-maximising individual. There may be many types of institutional constraints that prevent such rational settling at the margins. We are analysing government as a revenue-maximising monopolist, but not necessarily assuming it is a unique choice-making entity. The complexities of political decision-making are well known, and, in themselves, they may prevent the fine tuning reflected in some ideally rationalised portfolio adjustment procedure.

In the real world, government may simply be unable to invest in earning assets, almost regardless of the form of political structure – whether democratic or autocratic. Pressures upon governmental decision-makers to use up all revenues collected for direct consumption may be so strong as to forestall any accumulation of earning assets, quite independently of the discount rate preferred by the decision-makers. Even if, in one sense, this rate should be very low, or even zero, the investment-capital accumulation rules indicated by the simple relationship between such an internal rate and the rate of return on assets may not be carried out because of internal constraints in the political process itself (such as prohibitions on government investment in private securities).

Further than this, government may not find itself able to accumulate non-earning assets in any liquid form; hoarding as well as investment may be impossible. Government may be forced to spend all funds it has within single budget periods. Even if it cannot make portfolio adjustments like an individual, however, its rate of discount may still be such as to cause it to hold back from seeking confiscation of all the potential value of existing cash held by the public.

The permanence of the franchise

By all odds the most important element affecting the discount rate will be the anticipated length of the revenue franchise, whether for money-creation or other forms of revenue-raising. If government considers itself permanently entrenched, with no prospect of replacement or revolution, its decision-makers may take the long view, which would, of course, indicate a low rate of discount for the time-sequence of money-issue. (The same conclusion could be reached for all forms of taxation of capital.) The short-term prospects of getting real revenue by departing from any pre-announced path of money issue might be fully recognised, and the desirability of securing the goods that such revenues might purchase may remain intense, but government that thinks itself permanent will also recognise the long-term costs that loss of credibility would generate. The behaviour of a permanent monopoly government may, therefore, approach that of a government that finds itself externally constrained (either by moral precepts or constitutional law) to live by its commitments.

The continuing strain of such behavioural sequence should, however, be reckoned with. The prospects for short-term gains do not evaporate with one exercise of discipline; they continue to entice government in each and every period. And if and when government that has considered itself permanently installed in power modifies its perspective and sees a possible end to its franchise, the potential attractiveness of capital-value confiscation through inflation may come to dominate its behaviour.

Even with a permanent monopoly franchise, therefore, the citizens who make money-balance choices in the expectation that government promises will be honoured are taking a precarious leap of faith. If we shift attention to what we may call a 'temporary' franchise, the prospects for departures from monetary commitments are much higher. The government that sees itself in office or in power only for a fixed period will not reckon on the costs in loss of credibility during subsequent periods. It will have every incentive to inflate the money issue during the closing years of its reign, since it thus can confiscate the capital values represented in money balances at very little cost to itself.

Incentive to inflation of 'temporary' democratic government

The implications for the much-justified rotation of democratically elected governmental régimes are evident even if surprising. A government that knows itself to be a temporary holder of an effective monopoly franchise in money-creation will have every incentive to generate very substantial inflation during its terminal years. Given the same basic motivation for each of two governments, a continuing rotation in office of the two would be predicted to exploit the monopoly prospects of the money-creation franchise more fully than if either one of the two were placed in permanent office. In democratic electorates, the prospects for re-election and of citizens' historical memories of performances by governments will temper somewhat these seemingly paradoxical conclusions but not the direction of effect.

Our central subject is a revenue-maximising government. But suppose it maximises revenue only some of the time? Instead of the extreme assumption that all governments all the time behave as if they seek to secure the maximum gains from their monopoly franchise, let us assume that 'good' governments may exist, but that there remains always a probability that they will take on the revenue-maximising rôle. Suppose, for example, that an individual estimates that one government in three will act more or less as the maximiser of monopoly gains, and that it will use the money-issue franchise to maximise its command over real goods and services. The 'good' government that refrains from exploiting the monopoly potential of the franchise may then be of little or no value to the citizen. If he makes money-balance decisions on the basis of the observed behaviour of a 'good' government (behaviour that keeps money-issue in pre-commitment limits), he will be offering enhanced opportunities for the monopoly revenue-maximiser when and if it finally emerges in the political process. The citizen might be better off to remain highly cynical and to adjust his money-balance behaviour on the presumption that the revenue-maximising government *exists even when it does not*.

12 Revenue-maximising Inflation when Commitments are Honoured and when Individuals Expect Them to be Honoured

The analysis so far has suggested some of the difficulties that emerge in an attempt to define an individual's rational response in confrontation with a revenue-maximising monetary authority. We shall return to this central problem in Section 13. What of the behaviour of the revenue-maximising monopolist and of the individual on the presumption that any government undertaking to a money-issue sequence will be honoured, and that the individual acts as if he expects such government behaviour? What would the revenue-maximising calculus of the monetary authority be under this self-imposed constraint? What rate of inflation will it select?

This question has, perhaps surprisingly, been analysed relatively completely in the economics literature,[9] whereas most of the other questions raised in this *Hobart Paper* have been almost totally neglected, although they seem equally, if not more, important. The reason for this rather disproportionate treatment is attributable, at least in part, to the presumption that the analysis is more generally applicable than our structure suggests.

The costs to individuals of holding cash

The share of wealth an individual chooses to hold in the form of money balances will be related to the costs of holding them. The higher such costs are expected to be, the lower the real value of wealth that will be held in cash. The costs of holding cash balances are composed of two elements: the interest that the money holder could earn if he held his assets in the form of bonds or other non-money wealth rather than cash; and the reduction in the real value of his cash holdings that is associated with general inflation. (This latter 'cost' could, in principle, be a benefit if the government were to deflate so that the real value of cash rose over time.) The larger such 'costs', the smaller the cash balances people will hold, but the larger the revenue government can obtain from each £1 held. There will be some rate of inflation (new currency issue) that will maximise the total value to government of the money-issue franchise: applying that rate secures for government, in total, more real goods than the simple non-inflationary régime. This remains true even if the rate of inflation is announced in advance, if the monopolist lives by its promises, and if individuals believe it will do so. Or, in other words, even if the rate of inflation is fully anticipated by all potential holders of money, there will remain an incentive for government to select an inflationary rather than a non-inflationary régime.[10]

13 The Great Monetary Game

Some contributors to the orthodox discussion of this question examined the histories of great inflations in several countries and expressed some surprise that governments seem to have allowed (caused) rates of inflation far *exceeding* any plausibly computed revenue-maximising limits, given the fully anticipated, fully announced models of analysis. Why?

If government is studied as a monopoly, these results are not at all surprising. Indeed, our construction allows us to trace out a sequence. Government may decide to finance a portion of its future outlays by inflation, and announce its intention to generate a fixed rate of emission, with the initial purpose of living up to the commitment. As it issues the new money, however, it finds that it has severely over-estimated the quantity of real goods and services that can be financed by this method. Why are its estimates always likely to err in this direction? Because, quite simply, *individuals do not really expect governments to live by their promises*, and, therefore, hold *less* real balances than the amount projected for them by government. Government then finds it necessary to inflate the money supply *more* than it had projected in order to finance its spending commitments.

This '*strategic*' aspect of the interaction between government and individuals in money creation cannot, and should not, be overlooked or assumed non-existent. And rules for what is and what is not rational behaviour in such situations are not universally agreed upon. We have emphasised earlier the *impasse* between government and potential cash holders, and the difficulties of negotiating enforceable agreements. Another critical aspect of the money creation game now deserves some attention.

The monetary game is 'unfair'

The 'game' between the monetary authority and individuals is biased in favour of the government monopolist because of the elementary fact that individuals must make money-balance choices before the money-issue choices made by government in subsequent periods. It is as if one player in a game, the money franchise holder, is always allowed to 'go last' after the other player has made his commitment. It is hardly a 'fair' game.

It is this feature of the great monetary game – individuals must play first – that allows for the substantial degree of exploitation of the monopoly position. Individuals are not allowed to adjust their behaviour after they know what government is going to do about the money issue or even simultaneously with government's action. They are not allowed to react merely to an announcement, as they are normally allowed to do with an ordinary tax.

Tax on beer contrasted with 'tax' on money

Consider a tax on beer. Suppose government has been allowed to tax beer, which is equivalent to giving it a monopoly franchise in the sale of beer.[11] Individuals can adjust their behaviour in response to the tax-induced price increase; they can switch to wine without suffering substantial capital value losses over and above the amount they will pay in tax on the beer they choose to continue to purchase.

Contrast this sequence with the 'tax' on money that inflation represents. Individuals have made decisions to hold balances. Someone must continue to hold all the units of money in existence. There is no escape: the money previously issued must be held by somebody. Individuals may, and will, of course, choose to reduce the value of their money balances once they see that government is issuing new money. But the only way of accomplishing this result is to bid up money prices for goods. Hence, persons who hold money must suffer, necessarily, substantial capital losses on all previously held money balances.

It is in this sense that the inflation 'tax' on money balances is *retroactive*. It is this feature that makes such a 'tax' more closely analogous to a tax on capital assets than to a tax on any income or expenditure base. Individuals must make decisions to accumulate capital through time, and capital cannot be consumed immediately, once it has been accumulated. Hence, a tax on capital that is not anticipated long in advance can effectively confiscate capital values. Such a tax can yield revenues of more than 100 per cent of the income from the capital assets that are taxed. By comparison, 100 per cent of income is the absolute maximum revenue limit under an income tax.

What then is 'rational expectation' in the great monetary game between the monetary monopolist and individuals?[12] The upper limit on the monopolist's gain is set when all individuals continue to believe in every period that government has made its last issue of money. The lower limit is zero, when all individuals fully anticipate that the monopolist will move immediately to confiscate the full capital values of all real money balances and hence hold no balances in the form of money at all. For individuals, as potential holders and users of money, the upper limit on the benefits is the full transactions value in a non-inflationary régime, for which they would stand ready and willing to hand over to the monopolist.[13] The lower limit is the possibly very significant capital value confiscation that would emerge if individuals continued to act as if they believed the monopolist's pronouncements independently of its observed behaviour.

People learn to offset the actions of the inflationary monetary monopolist: towards a contractual approach?

The game is played between these limits. It seems plausible to suggest that different individuals in the economy will react differently. Some will presumably continue to be fooled for long periods; they will continue to add to and to hold real money balances in the face of continuing confiscation of values by inflation. The great hyperinflations in Hungary, Germany and other countries corroborate this statement.[14] To the extent that some individuals behave in this fashion, the monopolist has an enhanced incentive to inflate, despite the loss of value its behaviour may impose on persons who anticipate its action more accurately.

Through time, of course, as more and more people go through the learning process and come to predict the monetary issue policy of the government accurately, and as the real revenue gains from inflation approach zero, the incentive for government (as well as for individuals) to seek ways and means of devising some sort of enforceable agreement or contract to avoid the dilemma of the monetary game is increased.

14   Monetary Monopoly and Deposit Banking

Our analysis is based in the presumption that the government monopolist with the money-creation franchise is able to capture all the potential value ('monopoly rent') of such a franchise. In terms of a simple institutional structure, the analysis applies to an economy where the only monetary unit is the fiat currency (usually paper with no inherent value) issued by the governmental authority. In reality, such economies are rare. In most modern countries, fiat currency makes up only a part of the effective money in the economy. Fiat issue serves as a high-powered base for the derivative issue of bank money in the form of deposits. Can the analysis be applied to a monetary system that includes deposit banking as well as government fiat issue?

No difficulty arises if we suppose that the monetary monopoly sells the banking franchise to a single private firm in some sort of competitive auction process. The government would then capture the full value of all money issued just as if all the money were fiat. The analysis holds without qualification.

Can monopoly of money work with a competitive deposit banking system?

Problems seem to arise in competitive banking. How can the governmental monopolist then secure the potential value from bank-money creation? And, if it cannot do so, why should the governmental monopolist ever allow fractional-reserve banking to persist in which banks may create deposits in a stated multiple of reserves (as in the USA).

The introduction of fully competitive fractional-reserve deposit banking does not modify the real-revenue potential available to the fiat-issue governmental monopolist. Some share of the transactions value of money in the system will be returned to individuals as payment for their holding bank deposits. The opportunity cost (the yield on investments foregone) of holding money balances will be lower than under a régime in which no interest is paid on deposits. The public will hold more value in cash, for any given rate of inflation, than it will in a pure currency system. This difference allows the fiat-issue monopolist to generate a higher real-revenue maximising rate of inflation than under a pure fiat system. In effect, to the extent that fractional-reserve banking is competitive, our earlier analysis holds without qualification.

Reserve ratio control gives power to impose capital levies on banks

Fractional-reserve banking does, however, provide the monopoly government with one additional instrument of control. If it is legally authorised to change the required reserve ratio, the governmental monetary monopolist may be able to use this authority to impose what amounts to a capital levy on deposit holders (as in unexpected inflation, see below), without changing the rate of inflation.

If deposit banking is neither explicitly monopolistic nor fully competitive, if free entry into banking is not allowed, as it is not in many countries, banking charters or licences will, of course, be valuable, and, directly or indirectly, government can require payment for them.

15 Money Creation, Public Debt, and Income Taxes

So far, we have talked as if the sole effect of inflation on government revenue occurs through the financing of deficits by the creation of new money. This is an important and obvious aspect of inflation as a revenue device. But there are two other effects of inflation, both relevant for total government revenue yields and obligations.

The first is the effect of 'unexpected' inflation on the government's liabilities to service and redeem its interest-bearing debt. The second is the effect of inflation on personal income tax revenues. The significance of these less direct aspects of the revenue-implications of inflation may be, in total, at least as large in real terms as the matters that have been the focus of interest here.

All debtors, including government, benefit from unexpected inflation

Consider the effect on interest-bearing debt. Suppose the government has borrowed from private citizens an amount representing outstanding liabilities with a present value of, say, one million pounds in original prices. A once-and-for-all increase, say a doubling, in the money supply, totally unexpected but not expected to be repeated, will cause a reduction in the real liabilities represented by outstanding debt issue of half the total liability – half a million pounds in original prices. The reason is clear. Unexpected inflation redistributes real resources away from lenders to borrowers when all liabilities are specified in money values. To the extent that the government is a net borrower, it will gain when unexpected inflation occurs. In the example considered here, there will be no effect of the price increase on nominal interest rates because the increase in the money supply is not expected to be repeated.

If, on the other hand, the government made a once-and-for-all move from one 'permanent' inflationary régime to another, it would have to raise the nominal interest rate on all future debt issue. If the nominal interest rate rises so as to maintain the real rate (the nominal rate minus the rate of inflation, roughly), there would be no revenue advantage to government except in the period between régimes, which we take to be unexpected.

Therefore, except where government debt is indexed so that its real value to the private lenders is maintained despite inflation, essentially the same possibilities for revenue acquisition by government arise with interest-bearing debt as with non-interest bearing cash. The analysis of the effects of new money creation on the real wealth of holders of cash can be extended to include the real wealth of holders of government debt. The effect of inflation is to redistribute wealth from *both* private groups to government.

Inflation raises real government revenue from progressive income tax

The effects of inflation on the real value of income tax revenue are clear. The interaction of inflation with a progressive income tax structure increases *real* government revenue: inflation forces taxpayers into higher tax brackets and raises the average rate of tax for virtually everyone. (The exception is the group of taxpayers who after the inflation remain in the lowest bracket.)

This effect, although of considerable revenue significance, is quite different in its manner of operation from the effects of inflation on debt and cash holders. The taxpayer can, if he chooses, adjust his work and earnings *currently* to higher income tax rates, whether induced through inflation or discretionary legislative action; he can change jobs, refuse to work overtime, or refrain from seeking promotion to more arduous responsibilities, in response to higher effective income tax rates. He cannot so react if he is holding cash or government debt. In this sense, there is an important element of retroactivity in holding money-debt that is absent in paying income tax.

It is this element of retroactivity that renders the citizenry particularly vulnerable to exploitation *via* inflation, and that has consequently been the focus of our discussion here. It is this incapacity of the private citizen to avoid the oppressive monetary power of government that creates a case for a *monetary* constitution, even where explicit restrictions on income tax rates (or total tax revenues) are not considered desirable to enable him to avoid the oppressive fiscal power of government.

III The Implications for Policy

16 The 'Illegitimacy' of Unconstrained Monetary Monopoly

National governments' monopoly franchises in money creation are not normally constrained in any specific way. The analysis of part II, building on the political models developed in part I, offers convincing arguments that such unconstrained monopoly franchises are *illegitimate*, and that they should be recognised as such.

Having made this statement, we must define 'illegitimacy' and, by inference, 'legitimacy' quite carefully.[15] When we state that unconstrained monopoly franchises in money creation are 'illegitimate', we are implying that such monetary arrangements could not be derived as a legally justifiable part of the basic 'laws of the land', that is, of the constitutional order of a society. To justify such a statement, we must say what we mean by 'legally justifiable'.

Criteria for evaluating basic social/economic institutions

What are the ultimate criteria for evaluating the basic institutions of a desirable social order? If we reject the existence of (or at least general agreement on) external ethical norms such as those sometimes claimed to be present in 'natural law' or 'revealed religion', the criteria for evaluation of institutions must in some way be *derived from individuals themselves* as the only conscious, evaluating beings.

Individuals have their own identifiable interests, which may differ sharply among separate persons, families, groups, and social classes. How, then, can any generally applicable criteria be derived that will succeed in cutting through the conflicts among private or individual interests?

One means lies in removing the identification that the individual can make concerning his interest. If a person does not know either who he will be or, somewhat more realistically, how a particular legal institution will affect his interest, he will evaluate institutions in general terms instead of individualised interest.[16] Institutions or rules will tend to be selected so as to satisfy what has sometimes been called 'fairness' standards.

Viewed in this light, an institution stands the test of 'legitimacy' if it can be demonstrated that it could have been, or could possibly be, *agreed* on by all persons each of whom remains unable to identify the direct impact of that institution on his private interest. The contractural agreement that might be attained, or might have been attained, either behind the genuine Rawlsian 'veil of ignorance' or under the Buchanan/Tullock conditions of extreme uncertainty about the impact of institutions on individual interests, allows us to classify 'legitimate' and 'illegitimate' institutions for social order, including monetary arrangements.[17]

Voluntary agreement for unconstrained monetary monopoly would be impossible

The thrust of our argument is negative rather than positive. We claim that unconstrained government monopoly in money creation cannot emerge from a genuine constitutional calculus in which everyone participates and where individual positions are not identifiable or predictable. There may be several alternative monetary arrangements about which such a negative conclusion could not be reached, such as a commodity standard, a system of competitive monies, or fiat issue under constitutional constraints (several of these will be further discussed in Section 19). Any one of them may be preferred to unconstrained monopoly franchise, and we do not try to argue for any one from the many possible constitutionally acceptable alternatives. But progress in discussion will have been made if we can first secure agreement on what is *not* acceptable.

17 Legally Protected and Unconstrained Monopoly in Production or Sale

The argument may be generalised as well as exemplified by reference to any good or service that yields value in the economy, say, cornflakes (or milk, or apples). Suppose that an unconstrained but legally protected monopoly in the production and sale of cornflakes (or milk, or apples ...) should be proposed as an integral part of the institutional arrangements for society, and that this sort of proposal is taken under consideration at an initial stage of constitutional deliberation.

In the setting postulated for individual evaluation, individuals could not predict what their own positions might be on cornflakes. They will have no idea whether or not they might turn out to be consumers of cornflakes, owners of labour or capital used in the production and distribution of cornflakes, or recipients of the possible rents or profits that the holders of the cornflake franchise can expect to secure. They know only that the proposal before them involves the assignment of the rights to production and sale of cornflakes to a single individual or firm in the economy, that there will be no constraints on behaviour of the franchise-holder, and that the forces of the state will prevent the entry of potential competitors into the production and sale of cornflakes ....

Unregulated legal monopoly causes net social welfare loss

The first term in elementary economics is sufficient to suggest that ordinary people would never voluntarily agree to such an arrangement for monopolisation of the production and sale of cornflakes. They would reckon on the net welfare or efficiency loss that any such legally protected but unregulated monopoly franchise would generate, a net loss to the community that they would reckon on sharing, at least in part, since their individual position on cornflakes remains unidentified.

We can, of course, replace cornflakes (or milk, or apples) in all the above discussion by 'money', except for one important difference: there are far more opportunities for exploitation in a money-creation monopoly than there are with common-or-garden goods and services. In a real sense, money balances take the form of a capital good for which there is *no close substitute* in an economy: it is a 'natural' monopoly of a peculiar sort.

Natural monopoly and legal enforcement

But what about a standard 'natural monopoly'? Suppose our designated commodity, cornflakes ..., can be produced with economies of large-scale production.[18] The 'natural' forces of market competition would then evolve towards the domination of the whole cornflakes industry by a single firm, which would have an effective monopoly. If this tendency is recognised in advance, is there not an argument for legal monopoly, with the franchise granted through some device to the firm that might best qualify (through auction or otherwise)?

It is necessary to be clear on what such a grant of legal monopoly means. If it refers to governmental enforcement and protection against competitive entry of new firms into the industry, even when 'natural monopoly' exists, no such grant of legal monopoly can be justified unless it is accompanied by one that suggests simultaneous *enforceable limits or restraints* on the exercise of the sheltered monopolist's power. No argument for *unrestrained* legal monopoly is to be found even in the most naïvely-based support for special rights of 'natural monopolies'.

Two separate types of constraint on potential monopolistic behaviour must be distinguished.

First, potential or actual entry of competitors into an industry represents a restraint that is always present regardless of the dominating position of a firm *so long as there are no effective barriers to entry* enforced by government.

Second, if such barriers exist and potential entry exerts no restraint on behaviour, *regulation* may be designed to temper the degree of exploitation of the monopoly opportunity. The history of government intervention into the affairs of business allegedly designed to serve the 'public interest', such as in fuel and transport, education and health, provides ample evidence that all such businesses must accept the imposition of regulatory constraints in exchange for the grant of monopoly privilege.

18 Why Has Money Been Treated Differently?

'Natural monopoly' is one form of the 'market failure' argument. We have discussed the general 'market failure' arguments made by economists with reference to monetary arrangements (pp. 49–50). These arguments have been used to justify not only a governmental rôle in money matters, but also, and almost inadvertently, they have been extended to support the assignment of a *monopoly* right to create money by an agency or authority of government. We have suggested (pp. 51–3) there is no *prima facie* case for governmental intervention even if 'market failure' against some ideal is demonstrated. But our emphasis here is that, even if we provisionally accept some such justification, it cannot possibly extend to any support of the assignment of *unrestrained* monopoly power.

Economists have been uncritical of government monopoly in money

The very existence of monopoly franchises in money creation, which seem virtually free of explicit restraining rules, thus seems anomalous. Even stranger, perhaps, has been the relative paucity of economists' criticism of such institutional arrangements. Why has money somehow been assigned this special place?

We offer no fully satisfactory answer. The best we can do is our discussion of the benevolent-despot blindness that has created confusion among economists in their consideration of policy for a century. If the economist commences his task with the implicit presumption that governmental arms and agencies will at least try to 'do good', he will necessarily reject out of hand *any* enforceable constraint on governmental behaviour. He will, indeed, object (possibly strongly) to our whole monopoly construction in this *Hobart Paper* and elsewhere, whether we apply it to a monetary monopoly or to other governmental agencies. To such economists, there is really no meaning in efforts to define the limits to the exploitation of the monopolist's position, if the monopolist is benevolent by presupposition.

Even within the limits of the benevolent despot presumption, something seems amiss. There are many ways of 'doing good', and different political leaders motivated exclusively by their own interpretation of the 'public interest' will define their objectives differently. For many of these politicians, 'doing good' comes down to the spending of public monies. Hence, even for the most benevolent of politicians, revenue becomes a goal to maximise, an instrument through which they can promote happiness and well-being. Would it not then follow that, for such well-meaning politicians, revenue-*increasing* policy is to be preferred to revenue-*decreasing* policy? Would it not follow that, for such agents, inflation might still offer a very tempting source of gains?

Our brief and temporary acceptance of the heroic prospect that politicians may wish to promote the 'public interest' in their own lights, is perhaps sufficient to suggest that the argument against *unconstrained* grant of monopoly powers to any governmental agency of money issue does not critically depend on our extreme formulation of the revenue-maximising monopolist. It is, however, helpful in exposing 'natural' tendencies within government that can be disciplined by institutional–constitutional arrangements.

19 Monetary Arrangements to Meet Constitutional Tests

We have suggested that there may exist several institutional structures for ordering the monetary affairs of a community, any one of which may possibly qualify under our contractarian–constitutional test for acceptability. It may be conceptually possible for individuals to agree upon any one of such arrangements, which would then discipline unconstrained monetary monopoly. We do not propose to 'take sides' and to advance an argument in support of any of the arrangements that might meet the constitutional-agreement test. We present the alternatives and discuss each in summary to contrast the predicted working properties of those of unconstrained monopoly.

There are four régimes to be considered:

(1) *Free market in money, with no governmental rôle.* If unconstrained monetary monopoly is rejected as constitutionally unacceptable, there emerges essentially a two-stage question. Should government be assigned *any* rôle in ordering monetary affairs? And, if so, how should the powers be constrained?

Given adverse predictions about the operation of government in any rôle that might be assigned to it in running the supply of money, a constitutional evaluation may possibly suggest that the more desirable arrangement would be a totally free market in money, with no direct money-creating governmental rôle at all. The legal–political–governmental setting would require to be specified carefully, even here. We must presume that the government would be limited to minimal or protective state functions, largely involved in enforcing property rights and contracts among private parties.

There would then be no direct governmental rôle in money at all. The government would not define the medium of exchange; it would not print money; it would not regulate private printing of money or bank notes; it would not regulate banking or credit. Money would emerge, but exclusively as private money (or monies), with no government guarantees or repurchase arrangements. Government could, presumably, choose to collect taxes in the money or monies of its choice, just as private individuals might choose to make contracts in the money or monies of *their* choice.

Behaviour of government money monopolist crucial to choice between it and free markets in money

We earlier (pp. 49–50) sketched out economists' arguments that such free-market arrangements in money would tend to embody over-expansions and over-contractions. We are persuaded that these arguments, generally, are valid, and only a minority of economists would disagree. But even if we fully accept the 'market failure' analysis of free markets in money, they may be preferred to an unrestrained government monopoly.

The choice depends, in part, on a judgement of how the governmental authority would behave. If it is predicted that *any* assignment of a monetary rôle to government must inevitably degenerate into the unconstrained monopoly of money issue, the free-market argument becomes highly persuasive. It would amount to ruling out all the three other succeeding régimes as impracticable or implausible, although accepting that some initial constitutional prohibition would keep government totally out of the monetary picture.

(2) *Governmental money issue, but competitive entry.* A second régime that warrants examination is that which Professor Hayek seems to have in mind in his proposal for competitive monies. We could not expect any

government already possessed of a monopoly power to introduce and adhere to a régime that allows free entry into money creation. But we should consider the Hayek proposal seriously as a constitutionally selected set of monetary arrangements to guarantee such competitive entry.

In such a set of institutions, government may be empowered to issue domestic money, in whatever quantities it may choose. In this sense it would possess a monopoly franchise and it may be totally unrestrained in size of issue. The restraints present here, however, would emerge from the guarantee of free entry. The constitution would guarantee that individuals could hold balances, make private contracts, including the incurring of debts, and conduct ordinary transactions in any money of their choosing. This would open up the prospects for free entry, and citizens could use monies issued by foreign governments, commodity monies such as gold, or even paper monies issued by private firms and banks. The forces of competition would act as the restraint on the government money-issue monopoly, and if this agency attempted to exploit the profit potential of its position through inflation, its own money issue would quickly lose value.

The possible advantage of this set of arrangements over the totally free-market alternative lies in its incentives and sanctions for the government-issue monopolist to remain within non-inflationary bounds, whilst also offering some protection against the waves of expansion and contraction the free market might generate. The monopolist might recognise the potential for securing the transactions value of money in the economy, and individuals might also recognise the incentives for the monopolist to stay within pre-announcement limits.

(3)   *Pure commodity money, with governmental definition of value.* A third set of monetary institutions, various schemes for commodity or commodity-based money, is more familiar. The governmental rôle is limited to the definition of the monetary value of a physical unit of a designated commodity (or bundle of commodities in specified proportions). An ounce of gold of a specified degree of fineness is defined to be of, say, $400 in value, and the government 'opens its window' to sell and to purchase gold at this price. It does not create money on its own account; and if there is paper money it is convertible at a fixed price directly into the base commodity at the governmental money window.

The advantage of this arrangement is that the incentives of the profit-and-loss system are harnessed to generate stability rather than instability in the value of the monetary unit. If general price levels rise, while the value of the monetary commodity remains fixed, resources used in producing the money commodity become unprofitable; the rate of production falls, and the supply of money grows less rapidly, dampening the inflation in prices. On the other hand, if prices of non-money commodities fall, production of the money commodity becomes more profitable, leading to an expansion in the supply of money.[19]

The disadvantages of this set of institutions are twofold. First, the quantity of money is dependent on the elasticity of supply of the gold or other monetary commodity, and if this elasticity is low, there may be damaging lags in the working of the competitive forces.

Second, and perhaps much more importantly, any commodity-based monetary system tends to degenerate into a combination of an unrestrained government monopoly and an unrestrained free market in money. The goldsmith scenario (pp. 47–9) becomes directly relevant. Any pure commodity standard tends to become a commodity *reserve* standard, with potential profits to be exploited both by government and by private firms. Units of the money commodity, as such, would be used as reserves upon which derivative or 'low-powered' paper money would be issued. To police a commodity standard effectively, and to prevent such conversion into reserve usage of the money commodity, much governmental regulation over and above the mere definition of the value of the monetary unit would have to be laid down in the constitution.

(4)   *Fiat money issue constrained by constitutional rules.* Government may be empowered to issue money, and allowed a monopoly in it. But the constitution may subject the grant of the monopoly to specifically defined rules that limit the powers of the money-creation authority.

Two types of rules or directives command attention. First, a rule may specify directly-measurable quantities of nominal money. In the no-growth economy, the rule may specify that no money should be issued subsequent to an initial period. In a growing economy, the rule may state that the authority may expand the supply of money at a defined rate set at or near some projected rate of real growth in the economy. This type of rule is widely associated with Professor Milton Friedman, who has proposed it[20] both as an objective for discretionary government policy as well as a binding constitutional constraint. There may, of course, be several variants of a monetary growth rule, including one that specifies a range of rates for monetary growth rather than a single rate.

Monetary indexing for stability

A second rule may be defined in terms of ends rather than means. One such rule, advanced by Irving Fisher[21] and Henry Simons[22] among others, would direct the monetary authority to keep the value of the monetary unit stable, defined in terms of a designated index, which would require that the authority modify the quantity of money as necessary to accomplish this result. This rule, or some variant of it, has the advantage over the Friedman-like rule of allowing for flexibility in adjusting the quantity of money to an unpredicted emergence of money substitutes such as credit cards, but it is relatively more difficult to monitor than the money-growth type of rule. The monetary authority could be judged only after the event, when perhaps the damage had been done, and it would prove difficult if not impossible to distinguish genuine error from deliberate subversion of the rule.

20   The Three Stages of Monetary Debates

There are three separate stages of debate and analysis of monetary policy. These stages have not always been carefully distinguished one from the other, and controversies at one stage have tended to mask the basic agreement at others. In distinguishing among the three stages, we will indicate precisely where our discussion belongs.

1 Discretionary monetary policy

To the extent that political decision-makers have any latitude at all for discretion in their behaviour, the consequences of alternative courses of action may be analysed and discussed. The first stage of debates involves the week-by-week, month-by-month, year-by-year, or even government-by-government implementation of policy on monetary aggregates by the existing authority. The focus of the discussion is on what the legally-protected monetary monopolist 'should' do. What rate of expansion in the money supply should be followed? Should credit conditions be eased or tightened? Economists devote interminable effort to discussions of such questions without really understanding what rôle they are playing.

We do not suggest that the effort is wholly wasteful. Politicians and bureaucrats with decision-making power may pay some attention to the economists' arguments. But what must be recognised is that it is *persuasion* that is relevant, not the scientific validity or invalidity of this or that economic theory, not the moral superiority of this or that manner of behaving. Economists may impose some costs on the monetary monopolists by making them 'feel bad' by following their 'natural' tendencies towards generating real revenues through inflation, but these costs are likely to be dominated by the more direct incentives such as increased revenue. This predicted outcome will be emphasised by the recognition that not all economists will provide advice and counsel in the direction of lower rates of monetary expansion. Economists can always be found who will give evidence to support those directions of policy that coincide with the objectives of the real political revenue maximisers.

Our analysis and discussion in this *Paper* have little to do with this first stage of discourse.

2 The desirable monetary constitution

A second stage of analysis, discussion, and debate, that should be sharply separated from the first, involves consideration of alternative constitutional–institutional régimes, more or less along the lines of the earlier treatment (pp. 81–5). Proponents of totally free markets in money argue with those who support the establishment of a commodity-based money, or a return to a gold reserve standard, and both groups argue with those who advance proposals for constitutionally enforced money-growth or price-level stabilisation rules. Perhaps the most intense of such continuing arguments is that between the proponents of a gold-based commodity standard, the 'gold bugs', and the proponents of a fiat standard with constitutional safeguards.

The sharpness of the discord among the supporters and advocates of these two alternative régimes tends to overshadow and even negate the basic agreement among all these groups at a third level of discourse, that concerning the desirability of a monetary constitution itself.

3 The desirability of a monetary constitution

The proponents–advocates of free-market money, competitive monies, commodity money, or rule-constrained fiat issue *all* agree on the desirability, necessity, acceptability of *some monetary constitution*. Our argument in this *Hobart Paper* is exclusively devoted to this third stage. It is an argument for rules, in the familiar 'rules-versus-authority' debate. We have tried to be consistent in keeping clear of involvement in the other stages of the debates. We have not discussed alternative directions of monetary policy under discretionary authority of existing monetary monopolies.

We have offered no brief for one particular monetary constitution over others. Our charge is: Let us *first* agree that a monetary constitution is necessary *before* exhausting our energies in debates over the precise content of this constitution! Otherwise, the ship may sink while we debate which lifeboat to use.

Our brief is aimed to show that the absence of an explicit monetary constitution is unacceptable in any meaningful setting where the rules of social order are derived from the values held by citizens. To us it is indeed folly to confine analysis and discussion to examination of alternative lines of policy that are to be implemented by ordinary men and women who happen to find themselves in positions of political power. We should not, of course, deny that some such persons may be 'good men and true', but even victory in persuading one set of office holders to adopt 'our' preferred paths of monetary policy could only be short-lived.

Constitutional restraints, not 'advice', the only effective discipline on politicians

Experience should have taught us that direct economic advice to governments can be of relatively little lasting value. Men who make decisions in governmental rôles are ordinary mortals like the rest of us, and they will tend to be motivated by their own objectives instead of any 'truths' propounded by their economists. Once this simple point is recognised, our emphasis on *constitutional-institutional* change logically follows. Reforms in policy to be implemented by ordinary men can only come through reforms in the rules within which they operate.

We cannot, and should not, expect the decision-makers in the Bank of England or the United States Federal Reserve Board to behave 'as if' they are bound by a non-existent constitutional rule for money issue. They will behave in accordance with such a rule only if it exists. As the 1980s commence, more and more economists are coming to realise that unrestrained monetary monopoly is the *institutional* explanation of the great inflation of the 1970s. *Institutional* explanation suggests *insti-*

tutional reform. Only by restraining the discretionary powers of the monetary authorities through enforceable constitutional rules will the inflation be controlled. It is the *monetary régime*, not *monetary policy*, that must be modified.

Notes

1   A comprehensive discussion of this bias is in James M. Buchanan and Richard E. Wagner, *Democracy in Deficit: the Political Legacy of Lord Keynes*, Academic Press, New York, 1977; for an application to Britain, James M. Buchanan, Richard Wagner and John Burton, *The Consequences of Mr Keynes*, Hobart Paper 78, IEA, 1978.

2   For earlier works, James M. Buchanan and Gordon Tullock, *The Calculus of Consent*, University of Michigan Press, Ann Arbor, 1962; James M. Buchanan, *The Limits of Liberty*, University of Chicago Press, Chicago, 1975; James M. Buchanan, *Freedom in Constitutional Contract*, Texas A & M Press, College Station, 1978.

    A more thorough analysis which provides the basis directly for that of this *Hobart Paper* is in Geoffrey Brennan and James M. Buchanan, *The Power to Tax: Analytical Foundations of a Fiscal Constitution*, Cambridge University Press, Cambridge, 1980, and notably Chapter VI for a specific and more detailed analysis of the money-creation power.

3   This revenue-maximisation objective in application to all forms of revenue-raising, and not limited to money creation, is central to the analysis in our book, *The Power to Tax*, *op. cit.*

4   This notion of competing monies seems to be roughly what Professor F. A. Hayek has in mind, although apparently he would also allow private citizens, in addition to governments, to issue money. (*Denationalisation of Money*, Hobart Paper 70, IEA, 1976; 2nd edition, 1978.) Further discussion is in Part III.

5   In this and the following sections we shall assume that the money monopolist captures the full potential value of the franchise. In régimes that involve fractional reserve banking by non-governmental firms, the monopolist may or may not be able to capture the full value: further discussed in section 9.

6   Economist readers will recognise this scenario as that labelled as 'optimal' by Professor Milton Friedman. As our discussion perhaps suggests, the policy stance requires extremely naïve assumptions about the predicted behaviour of governments. Friedman was, of course, primarily concerned with the efficiency of the policy scenario, with efficiency defined in the strictest economic sense. (*The Optimum Quantity of Money and Other Essays*, Aldine, Chicago, 1969.)

7   This proposition is nothing more than another version of the neo-classical theorem about the stability of the 'Cambridge k', the share of wealth that individuals want to hold as cash balances. So long as tastes do not change, and so long as expectations about the value of money are stable, they will want to hold the same share of their total assets in the form of cash.

8   For the mathematically minded: the maximum present value, V, for the franchise in this model becomes:

$$V = M + M/(1+r) + M/(1+r)^2 \ldots = \frac{M}{r}.$$

Hence, the present value of the monopoly franchise in this setting is $\frac{1}{r}$ times the value in the non-inflationary régime.

9   For example, Martin Bailey, 'The Welfare Costs of Inflationary Finance', *Journal of Political Economy* 64, April 1956, pp. 93–110; Edward Tower, 'More on the Welfare Cost of Inflationary Finance', *Journal of Money, Credit and Banking* 9, November 1971, pp. 850–60.

10   For economists among our readers we can be somewhat more technical.

The demand for real balances falls as the costs rise. One point on the demand curve is that which is represented by the non-inflationary régime, where there is some initial quantity of money issued, M, along with the authority announcement that no subsequent issue will be forthcoming. (For analytical convenience here, we shall assume a no-growth economy. In an economy with real growth, new money may be issued proportionately to such growth while keeping prices stable.)

In the non-inflationary régime, the government gains the pure transactions value of money, M, but nothing more. It should perhaps be clear that this arrangement need not, and presumably will not, be that which maximises the present value of the franchise. The monetary authority will try instead to select precisely that rate of money emission (and inflation) through time that will maximise present value, given the presumed constraint that it must pre-announce the rate of emission in all subsequent periods and stick to its promises.

Differing rates of continuing and permanent inflation can be represented as different points along the demand curve for real balances, this time drawn for the whole community (see figure 1). The revenue-maximising position will be located where the elasticity of this curve is unitary. The rectangle subtended under the demand curve will measure present value of the franchise. We should note that, in this arrangement, the authority cannot gain as much real value in the initial period as it could under the non-inflationary régime. This result emerges because, with any positive rate of inflation that is fully anticipated, individuals will not use real goods to 'purchase' as much in real money balances as they would do under the non-inflationary régime.

Nonetheless, the present value of the franchise is higher under anticipated inflation than without because the present value of the anticipated and

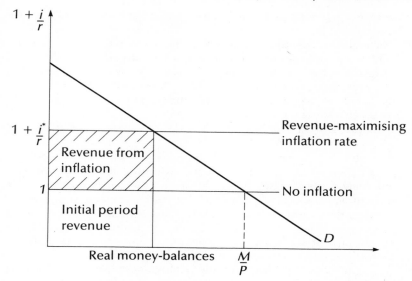

Figure 1 i = inflation rate; r = interest rate. D is the transactions demand for money.

announced rate of confiscation of capital values in real balances must be added on over and above the transactions value of the issue that can be gained in the first period.

11   *The Power to Tax, op. cit.*, elaborates this and related arguments.

12   One of the few examinations of the strategic aspects of the interaction between government and individuals is contained in Andrew Schatter and Gerald O'Driscoll, 'Why Rational Expectations May Be Impossible: An Application of Newcomb's Paradox', Discussion paper, Center for Applied Economics, New York University, November 1978.

13   We neglect the 'welfare triangle' that represents the added value that might be secured from a deflationary rate that just offsets the rate of return on real assets.

14   Philip Cagan, 'The Monetary Dynamics of Hyperinflation', in Milton Friedman (ed.), *Studies in the Quantity of Money*, University of Chicago Press, Chicago, 1956, pp. 25–117.

15   Our use of the terms 'legitimacy' and 'illegitimacy' may be unfamiliar to economists, but they will be recognised by political scientists and political philosophers who have discussed the 'legitimacy' and 'illegitimacy' of political institutions and of government for centuries. We have deliberately chosen to use these terms rather than milder ones such as 'acceptability' and 'unacceptability' because our application to the monetary arrangements

of society is precisely analogous to the broader application to government generally.

16   The evaluative procedure described briefly here, where the individual literally *does not know* who he will be, is a summary of the Rawlsian 'veil of ignorance' construction. (John Rawls, *A Theory of Justice*, Harvard University Press, Cambridge, Mass., 1971.) A less restrictive variant, where the individual may be able to identify himself but *cannot predict* how a particular institution will affect his interest, is developed in James M. Buchanan and Gordon Tullock, *The Calculus of Consent*, University of Michigan Press, Ann Arbor, 1962.

17   By suggesting that monopoly franchises in money creation are 'illegitimate', we are claiming basically that such arrangements could never have been, and could never be, agreed to *voluntarily* in a genuine social contract. In using such a 'contractarian' criterion for classification we are not, of course, implying that a genuine 'social contract' took place in history, or indeed that one could now take place. We claim only that the conceptual device of such a contract is used as a criterion for determining the possible acceptability of existing or proposed institutions or rules.

18   We are not concerned here with the validity of the hypothesis that such 'production functions' exist. We concentrate on the implications of the hypothesis 'as if' it were valid.

19   A general discussion of alternative constitutional money arrangements, with special discussion of commodity standards, is in Leland B. Yeager (ed.), *In Search of a Monetary Constitution*, Harvard University Press, Cambridge, Mass., 1962.

20   For example, in 'The Rôle of Monetary Policy', *American Economic Review*, March 1968, and *The Counter-Revolution in Monetary Theory*, Occasional Paper 33, IEA, 1970.

21   Irving Fisher (assisted by Harry G. Brown), *The Purchasing Power of Money*, Macmillan, New York, 1912.

22   Henry C. Simons, *Economic Policy for a Free Society*, University of Chicago Press, Chicago, 1948.

5

The Consequences of Mr Keynes

with R. E. Wagner and John Burton

I Democracy and Keynesian Constitutions: Political Biases and Economic Consequences

1 Visions of the Economic Order: Classical and Keynesian

The Classical or pre-Keynesian notions of prudent fiscal conduct were reasonably summarised by drawing an analogy between the state and the family. It was another British intellectual 'export', Adam Smith, who noted that 'What is prudence in the conduct of every private family, can scarce be folly in that of a great kingdom.' Prudent financial conduct by the state was conceived in basically the same image as that for the family. Frugality, not profligacy, was the cardinal virtue, and this norm assumed practical shape in the widely shared principle that public budgets should be in balance, if not in surplus, and that deficits were to be tolerated only in extraordinary circumstances. Substantial and continuing deficits were interpreted as the mark of fiscal folly. Principles of sound family and business practice were deemed equally relevant to the fiscal affairs of the state.

During this period, a free-enterprise economy was generally held as being characterised by 'Say's Equality'.[1] While fluctuations in economic activity would occur in such an economy, they would set in motion self-correcting forces that would operate to restore prosperity. Within this economic framework, the best action for government was simply to avoid injecting additional sources of instability into the economy. The profligacy of government was one latent source of disturbance, and it

Published originally as Hobart Paper No. 78, IEA (1978).

was considered important that this governmental proclivity should be restrained. Avoiding such sources of instability, along with keeping debt and taxes low so as to promote thrift and saving, was the way to achieve prosperity. A balanced or surplus budget was one of the practical rules that reflected such constraints and beliefs. Such siren songs as the 'paradox of thrift' were yet to come.[2]

From Classical stability to Keynesian instability

The idea that the spontaneous co-ordination of economic activities within a system of markets would generally produce economic stability was replaced in the Keynesian vision by the idea of an inherently unstable economy. Say's Equality was deemed inapplicable. The Keynesian paradigm was one of an economy alternately haunted by gluts and secular stagnation.[3] The prosperous co-ordination of economic activities was a razor's edge. The economic order is as likely to be saddled with substantial unemployment as it is to provide full employment. An important element in the Keynesian paradigm was the absence of an equilibrating process by which inconsistencies among the plans of the participants in the economic process became self-correcting. Prosperity, accordingly, could be assured only through deliberate efforts of government to help the economy avoid the buffeting forces of inflation and recession. 'Fine tuning' became the ideal of Keynesian economic policy.

The Keynesian message, in other words, contained two central features. One was the image of an inherently unstable economy, ungoverned by some 'natural law' of a generally smooth co-ordination of economic activities. The other was of government as having both the obligation and the ability to offset this instability so as to bring about a more smoothly functioning economic order. The notion of an unstable economy whose performance could be improved through the manipulation of public budgets produced a general principle that budgets *need not* be in balance: indeed, they *should not* be in balance, since that would mean government was failing in its duty. Some years of deficit and others of surplus were both necessary to, and evidence of, corrective macroeconomic management. A stable relation between revenues and expenditures, say a relatively constant rate of surplus, would indicate a failure of government to carry out its managerial duties.

2 The Idealised Environment for Keynesian Economic Policy

While Lord Keynes published his *General Theory* in 1936, his pre-suppositions did not infuse themselves into generally held understandings or beliefs for about a generation in America, though sooner in Britain, much as he anticipated in a famous passage on the time-lag between the articulation of an idea and its influence on policy.[4] While the Keynesian vision of the nature of our economic order and the proper pattern of budgetary policy gained dominance in academia in the 1940s and 1950s, it did not filter into the general climate of American opinion until the 1960s. With this conversion or shift in generally-held perspectives or beliefs, macro-economic engineering became the province of government.[5]

As developed by the economists who advocated macro-economic engineering, fiscal policy would be devoted to smoothing out cycles in private economic activity. Fiscal policy would be guided by the same principle during both recession and inflation. Deficits would be created during recession and surpluses during inflation, with the object of smoothing out peaks and troughs. The policy precepts of Keynesian economics were alleged to be wholly symmetrical. In depressed economic conditions, budget deficits would be required to restore full employment and prosperity. When inflation threatened, budget surpluses would be appropriate. The time-honoured norm of budget balance was thus jettisoned, but, in the pure logic Keynesian policy, there was no one-way departure. It might even be said that Keynesian economics did not destroy the principle of a balanced budget, but only lengthened the time-period over which it applied, from a calendar year to the period of a business cycle. In this way, rational public policy would operate to promote a more prosperous and stable economy during both recession and inflation.

While the idealised setting for the symmetrical application of Keynesian economic policy is familiar, the political setting within which the policy is to be formulated and implemented is much less familiar. We have now learned that mere exhortations to politicians to promote prosperity do not guarantee they will do so: they may lack the knowledge required to promote such an outcome, or the incentive to act in the required manner, or both. In other words, the actions of politicians on budgetary policy as well as on other types of policy depend upon both the knowledge politicians have and the incentives they confront.

Keynes's defective assumptions

Keynes largely begged questions pertaining to knowledge. Central to his approach was the presumption that economists could possess knowledge sufficient to enable them to give advice which, if acted upon, would facilitate the co-ordination of human activities within the economic order. This extremely questionable assumption about knowledge melded nicely with his normative assumptions about political conduct. Keynes was an élitist, and he operated under what his biographer called the 'presuppositions of Harvey Road' – that governmental policy, and economic policy in particular, would be made by a relatively small group of wise and enlightened people.[6] Keynes did not consider the application of his policy prescriptions in a contemporary democratic setting – in which government is tempted to yield to group pressures to retain or return to power. Rather, the small group of enlightened men who made economic policy would, he assumed, subconsciously – even if in defiance of historical experience – always tend to act in accordance with the 'public interest', even when this might run foul of constituency, sectional, or other organised pressures.

In the unreal economic and political environment envisaged by Keynes, there could be little or no question raised about the application of the Keynesian policy instruments. To secure a stable, prosperous economy, expenditures would be expanded and contracted symmetrically. Budget deficits would be created during periods of sluggish economic activity, and surpluses as the pace of economic activity became too quick. There would be no political pressures, he implicitly supposed, operating to render the surpluses fictional and deficits disproportionately large or ill-timed. The ruling élite would be guided by the presuppositions of Harvey Road; they would not act as competitors for electoral favour in a democratic political environment.

There was little awareness that the dictates of political survival might run contrary to the requirements of macro-economic engineering (assuming for now that the economic order is aptly described by the Keynesian paradigm). It was tacitly assumed either that the political survival of politicians was automatically strengthened as they came to follow more fully the appropriate fiscal policies, or that the ruling élite would act without regard to their political fortunes. But what happens when we make non-Keynesian assumptions about politics? What if we commence from the assumption that elected politicians respond to pressures emanating from constituents and the state bureaucracy? When this shift of perspective is made in the political setting for analysis, the possibilities that policy precepts may unleash political biases cannot be ignored. On this score, it should be noted that Keynes's own biographer seemed prescient, for in continuing his discussion of the presuppositions of Harvey Road, he mused:

> If, owing to the needs of planning, the functions of government became very far-reaching and multifarious, would it be possible for the intellectual aristocracy to remain in essential control? Keynes tended till the end to think of the really important decisions being reached by a small group of intelligent people, like the group that fashioned the Bretton Woods plan. But would not a democratic government having a wide multiplicity of duties tend to get out of control and act in a way of which the intelligent would not approve?
>
> This is another dilemma – how to reconcile the functioning of a planning and interfering democracy with the requirement that in the last resort the best considered judgement should prevail. It may be that the pre-suppositions of Harvey Road were so much of a second nature to Keynes that he did not give this dilemma the full consideration which it deserves.[7]

3 Keynesian Presuppositions, Democratic Politics, and Economic Policy

Anyone, citizens no less than politicians, would typically like to live beyond his means. Individual citizens generally face a personal or household budget constraint which prevents them from acting on this desire, although some counterfeit and others go bankrupt. In the century before the shift in belief wrought by the Keynesian revolution, politicians acted as if they sensed a similar constraint when making the nation's budgetary choices.

Contemporary political institutions, however, are constrained differently because of the general belief in the Keynesian vision. This shift in constraints due to the shift in general beliefs alters the character of governmental budgetary policy. While there is little political resistance to budget deficits, there is substantial resistance to budget surpluses. Hence, fiscal policy will tend to be applied asymmetrically: deficits will be created frequently, but surpluses will materialise only rarely. This bias results from the shift in the general, public impression or understanding of the Western economic order, and of the related rules of thumb held generally by the citizenry as to what constitutes prudent, reasonable, or efficacious conduct by government in running its budget. Old-fashioned beliefs about the virtue of the balanced-budget rules and of redeeming public debt during periods of prosperity became undermined by Keynesian ideas, and lost their hold upon the public. In consequence, debt reduction lost its claim as a guiding rule. Budget surpluses lost their *raison d'être*. Deficits allow politicians to increase spending without having directly and openly to raise taxes. There is little obstacle to such a policy. Surpluses, on the other hand, require government to raise taxes without increasing spending – a programme far more capable of stimulating political opposition than budget deficits, especially once the constraining norm of debt retirement had receded from public consciousness.

Market and political competition: similarities and essential differences

In a democracy, political competition bears certain resemblances to market competition. Private firms compete among themselves in numerous, complex ways to secure the patronage of customers. Politicians compete among themselves for the support of the electorate by offering and promising policies and programmes which they hope will get them elected or re-elected. A politician in a democratic society, in other words, can be viewed as proposing and attempting to enact a combination of expenditure programmes and financing schemes that will secure him the support of a majority of the electorate. This realistic view of the formulation of economic policy in a political democracy found no place in Keynes's *General Theory*. Its absence made his policy proposals unsound, because unrealistic.

There are also, it is worth noting, important differences between market and political competition. Market competition is continuous; at each purchase, a buyer is able to select among competing sellers. Political competition is intermittent; a decision is binding generally (as in the USA) for a fixed number of years. Market competition allows several competitors to survive simultaneously; the capture by one seller of a majority of the market does not deny the ability of the minority to choose their preferred supplier. Political competition leads to an all-or-nothing outcome: the capture of a majority of a market gives the entire market to that supplier. Again, in market competition, the buyer can be reasonably certain as to just what it is that he will receive from his purchase. In political competition, the buyer is in effect purchasing the services of an agent, whom he cannot bind in matters of specific compliance, and to whom he is forced to grant wide latitude in the use of discretionary judgement. Politicians are simply not held liable for their promises and pledges as are private sellers. Moreover, because a politician needs to secure the co-operation of a majority of politicians, the meaning of a vote for a politician is less clear than that of a 'vote' for a private firm. For these reasons, among others, political competition is different from, and inferior to, market competition, even though there is a fundamental similarity.[8] This was generally overlooked in economic analysis until recent years, and entirely ignored by Keynes and the Keynesians who followed him.

Budgets: political gains and losses

The essential feature of democratic budgetary choice may be illustrated by considering the gains and losses to politicians of supporting various-sized budgets, and the taxes and expenditures they entail. It is the expectation of political gains and losses from alternative taxing and spending programmes which shapes the budgetary outcomes that emerge within a democratic system of political competition. The size and composition of public budgets in such a system of competitive democracy can thus be viewed as a result of the preferences of a politician's constituents and the constitutional–institutional rules that constrain the political system.

With a balanced-budget rule, any proposal for expenditure must be coupled with a proposal for taxation. The elimination of the balanced-budget rule as a result of the advent of the Keynesian revolution altered the institutional constraints within which democratic politics operates. The nature of the pressures of political competition consequently would differ in this revised, Keynesian constitutional setting from what they were in the Classical constitutional setting. What we must do now is consider the respective survival prospects of budget surpluses and budget deficits, showing in the process that deficits have stronger political survival value than surpluses once the Keynesian vision and its concomitant beliefs replaced the Classical vision.

Budget surpluses and democratic politics   Assuming an initial situation of budget balance, the creation of a budget surplus requires an increase in real rates of tax, a decrease in real rates of public spending, or some combination of the two. In any event, budget surpluses will impose direct and immediate costs on some or all of the citizenry. If taxes are increased, some persons will have their disposable incomes reduced. If public spending is reduced, some beneficiaries of public services will suffer. In terms of *direct* consequences, a policy of budget surpluses will create losers among the citizenry, but no gainers.

Gainers must be sought for in the *indirect* consequences of budget surpluses. There may be some general acceptance of the notion that the prevention of inflation is a desirable objective for national economic policy. It could be argued that people should be able to see beyond the direct consequences of budget surpluses to the *indirect* consequences. They should understand that a budget surplus was required to prevent inflation, and that this was beneficial. The dissipation of a surplus through public spending or tax cuts, therefore, would not be costless, for it would destroy the benefits that would result from the control of inflation.

These direct and indirect consequences act quite differently on the choices of typical citizens. The direct consequences of the surplus take the form of reductions in *presently enjoyed consumption*. If taxes are raised, the consumption of private services is reduced. If government spending is lowered, the consumption of government services is reduced. In either case, a budget surplus requires citizens to sacrifice services they are consuming.

The indirect consequences, on the other hand, are of an altogether different nature. The benefit side of a budget surplus is not directly experienced, but rather must be *imagined*. It takes the form of the hypothetical or imagined gains from *avoiding* what would otherwise have been an inflationary experience.[9]

A variety of evidence suggests that these two types of choices are psychologically quite different. Moreover, appreciation of the benefits from a budget surplus would require a good deal of information and understanding. The task is not a simple matter of choosing whether to bear $100 more in taxes this year in exchange for $120 of benefits in two years, and then somehow comparing the two, historically distinct, situations. The imagining process requires an additional step. The person must form some judgement of how he, *personally*, will be affected by the surplus; he must reduce his estimate of the total ('macro-economic') impact of the surplus to a personal ('micro-economic') level. As such future gains become more remote and less subject to personal control, however, there is strong evidence to suggest that such future circumstances tend to be neglected. 'Out of sight, out of mind' is the common-sense statement of this effect.[10]

Budget surpluses clearly have weaker survival prospects in a political democracy than in a social order controlled by a set of Keynesian wise men following the presuppositions of Harvey Road. Budget surpluses may emerge in a democratic political system, but democratic political processes possess institutional biases against them. Viewed in this light, there really should be no difficulty in understanding why we have never observed the explicit creation of budget surpluses during the post-Keynesian years.

Budget deficits and democratic politics   In a democratic society, there would be no obstacles to budget deficits in a Keynesian economic setting. Budget deficits make it possible to spend without taxing. Whether the deficit is created through reduced taxes or increased expenditures, the form each takes will, of course, determine the distribution of gains among citizens. The key difference from a budget surplus, however, is that there are only direct gainers from such deficits and no losers.

Deficits will also create losers indirectly, due to the resulting inflation. Such indirect consequences are, however, dimensionally different, as we have seen. The direct consequences of debt creation take the form of increased consumption of currently enjoyed services; these would be privately provided services if the deficit took place through a tax reduction, and government-provided services if through an increase in government expenditure. The indirect consequences, however, relate not to present experience, but to future conjecture. The benefit of deficit finance resides in the increase in currently enjoyed services, whereas the cost resides in the inflationary impact upon the future, in the creatively-imagined reduction in well-being at some future date. The analysis of these indirect consequences is essentially the same as that of the indirect consequences of the budget surplus.

A democratic society, therefore, will tend to resort to an excessive use of deficit finance once acceptance of the Keynesian paradigm has led to a revision of the fiscal constitution. For this reason, the post-Keynesian record in fiscal policy is not difficult to understand. The removal of the balanced-budget principle of constitutional rule generated an asymmetry in the conduct of budgetary policy in our form of competitive democracy. Deficits are created, but to a larger extent than justified by the Keynesian principles; surpluses sometimes result, but they occur less frequently than required by Keynesian prescriptions. When plausible assumptions are made about the institutions of decision-making in political democracy, the effect is to increase the biases against the use of budgetary adjustments to prevent and control inflation, as well as to increase the bias toward budgetary adjustments aimed at stimulating spending.

Keynesian economics in political democracy   The grafting of Keynesian economics onto the fabric of a political democracy has wrought a significant revision in the underlying fiscal constitution. The result has been a tendency toward budget deficits and, consequently, once the workings of democratic political institutions are taken into account, inflation. Democratic governments will generally respond more vigorously in correcting for unemployment than in correcting for inflation. Budgetary adjustments aimed at the prevention or control of inflation will rarely be observed as the result of deliberate policy. Budget deficits will come to be the general rule, even when inflation is severe. In slack years, when deficits might seem warranted by strict application of the Keynesian precepts, the size of these deficits will become disproportionately large. Moreover, the perceived cost of government will generally be lower than the real cost because of the deficit financing. As a consequence, there will also be a relative increase in the size of the government sector in the economy. Budget deficits, inflation, and the growth of government – all are intensified by the Keynesian destruction of former constitutional principles of sound finance.

4 The Destructive, Self-fulfilling Character of the Keynesian Political Biases

These political biases towards budget deficits also become a bias towards inflation, because monetary institutions as they are currently constituted operate, to some extent, to increase the stock of money in response to budget deficits. The one-sided application of Keynesian policy precepts which emerges from a democratic political setting may itself create economic instability in the process.

While inflation is usually thought of as a *proportionate* rise in all prices, as a rise in the absolute level of prices, in practice the structure of *relative* prices changes as well.[11] Indeed, what are commonly referred to as macro-economic policies are not instruments intended to influence all prices proportionately, but rather are instruments intended to influence the structure of *relative* prices. The dictates of political survival operate in this direction because it is only through policies designed to act on relative prices that the vote-buying activities of politicians and parties can take place. A macro-economic policy aimed only at the general price level would be typified by an indiscriminate dropping of money from a helicopter.[12] But any such non-discriminatory policy would be defeated politically by a policy designed to benefit specific recipients, such as a spending programme in marginal constituencies. In other words, the primary phenomenon to be considered in examining the inflationary bias of Keynesian economics is not the level of absolute prices, but rather the change in the structure of relative prices. Macro-economic consequences are simply the sum of these micro-economic consequences.[13]

Once it is recognised that the important consequence of inflation is its impact on relative prices, and particularly once it is recognised that rational political action would aim at selective shifts in relative prices rather than at non-selective shifts in absolute prices, a new perspective on the destructive character of the Keynesian political biases emerges.[14] This is particularly true once it is also recognised that the essential nature of the economic order is vastly different from that implied by the standard treatments on inflation and macro-economic policy. In these standard treatments the economy is viewed much like a balloon. Blow and the economy expands; suck and it contracts. This vision of the economy inherent in most macro-economic models makes it appear to be a simple matter to achieve both the desired *degree* of inflation or contraction and the desired *timing* of those expansions and contractions.

Such a view of the economic order, while making life easy for econ-omists, hardly conforms to economic experience. Rather, an economy is a complex web of contractual relations that reflect the anticipations and plans of the various participants. Metaphorically, it is far more like a gigantic erector set running throughout a 200-room mansion, with each piece connected to pieces in many different rooms. Changes made at one point will exert effects throughout the system, and will do so with varying time delays. *And no one person will be able to apprehend the entire apparatus*, quite unlike the case of the balloon. Moreover, shifts taking place at one point can be the consequence of earlier shifts elsewhere, and there is no assurance about the consequences of additional changes made at that point.

Today's economic occurrences and disturbances are a complex, only partially apprehendable result of previous changes in many places at many different times in the past. Thus, the injection of new changes in budgetary policy is quite unlike inflating or deflating a balloon.[15] It is rather like readjusting some of the particular links in the erector set, only the metaphor should be even more complicated because the indi-vidual nodes have a will, so, therefore, they can think, create, and act.[16] These readjustments will disturb a whole set of anticipations and plans, with the consequences of these readjustments extending over various periods.

Hayek's analysis of the impact of inflation

There are several facets to the story about how the shifts in relative prices, induced by inflation, can have dis-co-ordinating impacts upon our economic order. One was articulated by Professor F. A. Hayek in the 1930s.[17] The initial impact of the inflation in Hayek's analysis was to shift the structure of relative prices in favour of capital goods of long gestation periods. The resultant lengthening of the structure of production, however, is inconsistent with the underlying data of wants, resources, and knowledge. Such a pattern of employment and output cannot be maintained without an acceleration of the inflation. But a continually accelerating inflation is not sustainable as a long-run feature of an economic order. In the absence of such acceleration, the structure of production will revert to its former state. This process of readjustment leads to unemployment and recession. A recession becomes a necessary price of the *political* activities that produced the inflation in the first place, unless some movement toward an incomes policy to repress the inflation takes place, in which event the distortions would simply manifest themselves somewhat differently. Reallocations of labour must take place before the economy's structure of production will once again reflect the underlying data to which the economy adapts. Thus people respond to non-sustainable price signals generated by the inflation, and the resulting mistakes must be worked out before the economy can return to normalcy. Recession is an inherent part of the recovery process.

In Hayek's framework, the excessive expansion occurred in the capital goods industries. In these days of massive government spending, however, the story is more complex, for it is the activities on which politicians increase spending that generate an excessive absorption of resources. This attraction of resources due to the shift in relative prices need not be confined to the capital goods industries, because there can be other industries that will be differentially favoured by the government spending policies. Nonetheless, the central consequence remains: a pattern of resource allocation will be brought about that is not sustainable without still further efforts at distorting the structure of relative prices through inflationary finance. The Keynesian inflationary biases can be considerably more destructive than a simple increase in the general price level, because the changes in relative prices lead to further distortions as people act on the basis of price signals that are inconsistent with the underlying structure of preferences and technology. As a result of these mistakes, decisions will be made on investment and the employment of resources that are not sustainable by the economy. Unemployment and capital waste will then result as people readjust their plans and actions to correct mistakes based on erroneous signals in the economy.

5 Conclusion

Why does Camelot[18] lie in ruins? Intellectual error of monumental proportion has been made, and not exclusively by the politicians. Error also lies squarely with the economists. The 'academic scribbler' who must bear substantial responsibility is Lord Keynes, whose thinking was uncritically accepted by establishment economists in both America and Britain. The mounting historical evidence of the ill-effects of Keynes's ideas cannot continue to be ignored. Keynesian economics has turned the politicians loose; it has destroyed the effective constraint on politicians' ordinary appetites to spend and spend without the apparent necessity to tax.

Sober assessment suggests that, politically, Keynesianism represents a substantial disease that over the long run can prove fatal for the survival of democracy.

II Constitutional Options for Fiscal Control

6 Fatalism versus Reform

This *Hobart Paper* has sought to explain why the acceptance of Keynesian economics in a democratic society leads to an inflationary bias, and why the destructive economic consequences that spring from it can make the erroneous Keynesian analysis of our economic order take on the appearance of a self-fulfilling prophecy. We should not be surprised at the contemporary fiscal and economic record. Once the last vestiges of the Classical norm of the balanced budget were removed, nothing was left to constrain the spending proclivities of politicians, and, indirectly, those of voters themselves.

Two means of improvement might suggest themselves. We might acknowledge that policies derived from Keynesian economics cannot be applied within representative democracy. Some might go on to suggest that basic choices on macro-economic policy should be taken away from the decision-making power of ordinary politicians and entrusted to a small group of 'experts', 'economic technocrats', 'planners', who would, it is assumed, be able to 'fine tune' the national economy in accordance with the true 'public interest' and wholly free of political interference. This naïve approach begs all questions concerning effective incentives for the 'experts', and ignores the demonstrated informational difficulties in forecasting and controlling. Various arguments for incomes policies and national economic planning, which now seem to be re-emerging, represent in reality an effort to replace our democratic political institutions with non-democratic institutions more consonant with the Keynesian presuppositions.

From a democratic point of view, there are strong objections to any such removal of decision-making power from our elected representatives. Recognition of the political biases we have described, along with a commitment to the basic values of representative democracy, leads necessarily to a consideration of the fiscal constitution, which defines the set of constraints within which elected political representatives operate. In this perspective, the acceptance of the Keynesian paradigm, misplaced in its analytical foundations, has led to the destruction of one important element of this constitution that has not been replaced. The spending and inflating proclivities that have been unleashed are capable of making the economy appear to conform to the Keynesian view of the world.

Politicians will be politicians, one might say. And bureaucrats will be bureaucrats, one might add. Together, in the absence of constitutional constraints, they possess enormous potential for economic destruction. Much of the vote-buying activities of politicians have been passed off as necessary to promote a more effectively working economy. And who would want to promote a *less* effectively working economy? But such unrestrained political actions lead to economic instability, which is then used to justify further political efforts to 'stabilise' the economy. So sails the ship of state. To call for further helmsmanship from the pilots who have exacerbated our troubles in the first place would be logical only for those who enjoy being seasick or like long-distance swimming, but it is not a 'remedy' that many of us would anticipate with much enthusiasm. A combination of a rule for fixed monetary growth and a rule for a balanced government budget would go far in checking governmentally induced sources of instability. Must we continue to trust short-run steering of an otherwise stable ship to an inherently biased helmsman, and then blame the subsequent instability upon the ship itself?

Force the helmsman to stop fiddling with the tiller?

The prospects for fiscal reform may not seem bright; that should not make us fatalists or determinists. As with the vision of Charles Dickens's Spirit of Christmas Yet-to-Come, prospects look bleak only if existing bad habits – modes of fiscal conduct – are continued. It is precisely because we see not one inevitable projection of history but rather alternative histories that might unfold, and which will unfold as a result of choice and the exercise of intelligence, that we see hope. That hope is that through the explanation of the harmful consequences of present harmful policies we shall adopt courses of action that allow us to escape from them.[19] As people come to understand more accurately the source of the curse that plagues them, fiscal conduct will change. We are engaged in a process in which the explanation of social phenomena alters our understanding of our self-interest, thereby modifying human conduct and social phenomena. We therefore believe that the recent signs of concern about the conduct of budgetary policy under our constitutional framework, of which this *Paper* is one expression and *Democracy in Deficit* is another, will contribute to this needed shift in understanding and, as a result, in budgetary policy.

7 Concrete Proposals for the Reform of the British Fiscal–Monetary Constitution

The historic rôle of the House of Commons was that of opposing a revenue-hungry Crown under the banner of 'no taxation without representation'. It now faces a new challenge, from a new sovereign, and it needs another banner: 'No economic manipulation for political profit'.

What concrete proposals can be offered for the reform of Britain's monetary–fiscal constitution?

(1) *A combined budget statement.* Britain is one of the few Western countries in which government spending proposals are considered

separately from its revenue proposals.[20] This practice has arisen as the unintended consequence of parliamentary rules of procedure adopted in the 19th century. A change in these procedures is necessary. The two sides of the fiscal situation should be considered jointly, to emphasise the essential link between them.

But this measure would not in itself eradicate the flaws of the present fiscal constitution. It would simply remove a procedural anachronism.

(2) *Re-adopt the balanced budget principle* (preferably in writing). The central problem must be faced squarely. The present British fiscal constitution contains a bias towards persistent budgetary deficits, and permits the manipulation of the economy for short-term political profit. The economic consequences are unremitting and volatile inflation, unending growth of government expenditure, and a continuous erosion of the effective functioning of the price system. If these conditions persist, the ultimate survival of British democracy itself will be at stake.

If Britain is to avoid this grim folly, government must be subjected to a constitutional rule that eradicates its ability to manipulate the fiscal system and the economy for political profit. The rule should also be simple, clear, workable, and comprehensible to the general public. No public purpose is served in beating about the bush on this issue. *The only constitutional rule that fulfils these criteria is the principle of the balanced budget.*

But a return to the previously-unwritten constitutional convention of the balanced budget may not now be sufficient. Mere conventions, once broken, are too easily broken again. A written constitutional rule, rather than a convention, is therefore now called for. The House of Commons must adopt a new Standing Order:

> This House requires that total government expenditure does not exceed total government revenue from taxation and charges.

(3) *Automatic adjustment towards budget balance.* Even though required by the House of Commons to adopt a balanced budget, government could present in its Budget Statement only a *projected* equality of its revenues and expenditures over the forthcoming fiscal year. Given the inherent difficulties of forecasting these magnitudes accurately, discrepancies would be bound to emerge over the fiscal year. How then is budget balance to be maintained?

A constitutionally defined *adjustment rule* is necessary to specify what should happen. If a budget deficit occurs, either expenditure must be reversed downwards to match revenue, or revenue must be increased to match outlay. Furthermore, the adjustment rule must be triggered automatically, by the emergence of a differential between outlay and revenue over and beyond some given threshold. The acceptance of a clear, automatic and obligatory adjustment rule is more important than the specific character of the rule adopted. Our specific proposal is that, if budget projections prove to be in error, and a budget deficit larger than a specified (small) limit emerges, government expenditure must be adjusted downward to restore projected balance within a period of three months. If a budget surplus emerges, the excess funds must be used to retire (i.e. reduce) the National Debt.

The adopted adjustment rule would also need to be codified as a House of Commons Order.

(4) *Orderly transition to full implementation.* To eradicate the budget deficits of recent British vintage within one fiscal year would result in economic upheaval. To minimise these adjustment problems (they cannot be eradicated entirely), the goal of budget balance should be approached in stages over a number of years. Our specific suggestion is that orderly transition requires that annual budget deficits be reduced by not less than 20 per cent in each of the five years subsequent to the adoption of the balanced-budget constitutional rule. Departure from this transition programme would be treated in the same manner as departure from budget balance upon full implementation: the automatic adjustment rule would be triggered.

(5) *Waiver in national emergency.* A waiver clause in the House of Commons Order on budget balance is necessary to deal with national emergencies, such as wars or financial crises. The purpose of a balanced-budget rule is to extirpate the biases and consequences of the present fiscal constitution that exist even in conditions of economic normalcy. It should not prevent recourse to government borrowing under the abnormal conditions of a genuine national emergency. Our specific proposal is that if the majority party (or coalition) holds less than two-thirds of all seats in the House of Commons, the rule of budget balance may be waived if two-thirds of MPs so vote. This waiver clause would be sufficient to deal with the typical post-war situation, in which no governing party has commanded more than two-thirds of the seats in the House. If it ever did, the waiver clause would have to be strengthened, to restrain the potential manipulation of the economy by the Executive for political profit. Our specific proposal is that, if the governing party

or coalition holds more than two-thirds of parliamentary seats, the balanced-budget rule may be waived only if a third or more of the remaining, non-governing-party MPs so vote with government-party MPs.

(6)   *Conditions for monetary stability.* This *Paper* has concentrated on the fiscal side of the fiscal–monetary constitution. But monetary and fiscal actions are in practice closely intertwined. We have argued for *fiscal* stability; we do not deny that a similar importance attaches to the maintenance of *monetary* stability.

The Bank of England has apparently moved, over recent years, towards acceptance of the monetarist view that the rate of increase of the money supply should be low and regular. But this change of attitude is not in itself a sufficient guarantee of monetary stability. The Bank has no statutory objectives, and final authority over monetary policy is retained by government, which also appoints the Governor of the Bank. It is these conditions that must be changed if there is to be a credible guarantee of monetary stability. First, the Bank of England must be made statutorily independent of the government, as advocated by the Editor of *The Times*, Mr William Rees-Mogg.[21] Second, the Bank must be required by statute to adopt a fixed and specific rule for the rate of growth of the money supply. As with the fiscal adjustment rule, the precise nature of this rule is less important than the basic principle that a fixed and clear rule is adopted. Our specific proposal is that the rate of growth of the monetary base – the key quantity which determines the rate of growth of the total money supply – should be maintained at a constant rate, equal to the average rate of growth of real gross domestic product over (say) the last three decades.[22]

The House of Commons would also have the right to waive this rule, in times of national emergency, under the same conditions as (5) above.

The difficulty that Parliament faces in seeking to impose these new constitutional rules should not be minimised. For the People's House to battle against an external privileged minority, such as the Crown or the Lords, is one thing. It must now seek to check a new sovereign that sits in its midst, and which controls it. It is to be hoped that this *Paper* will contribute to that difficult task.

8 Unfounded Fears

The main worry that some might voice about our proposals is that 'Life without Keynes' would mean a return to the inter-war slump. This fear is completely without foundation.

First, there is simply no evidence to suggest that market economies are inherently unstable. Econometric research has shown that market economies are dynamically stable.[23] The business cycle does not arise because of any inherent instability on the part of the economy, but apparently is caused by exogenous 'shocks' that disturb its workings.

Second, the evidence indicates that the most serious 'shocks' that destabilise the economy are ill-considered and erratic policy actions *by government*. The tragedy of the inter-war slump illustrates this fundamental truth. Winston Churchill's decision in 1925 to return to the gold standard at the pre-World War I parity has been correctly described as 'the most important single act of economic policy in the decade of the 'twenties'.[24] The massive shock it administered severely destabilised the British economy. This decision was bitterly attacked by Keynes in a pamphlet entitled *The Economic Consequences of Mr Churchill*; to his credit, Churchill himself later came to view his decision as the most serious mistake of his life.[25] The Great Contraction of the 1930s in the USA likewise owed its origins to inept decisions, in this case by the Federal Reserve Board (the US monetary authority). The historical research of Professors Milton Friedman and Anna J. Schwartz have revealed that from 1929 to 1932 the US money supply (defined here to include time deposits) fell by 35.2 per cent.[26] While some part of this catastrophic decline may be partly accounted for by falling economic activity, there can be no doubt that it was primarily caused by the inaction of the Federal Reserve at the beginning of the episode, and its incorrect handling later on. The Federal Reserve, supposedly designed to prevent banking crises, instead caused one.

The general lesson is that slumps are *not* due to the supposedly unstable nature of the market economy. They are the unfortunate consequence of external 'shocks' impinging on the economic system: primarily ill-considered acts of government policy.

A régime of fiscal and monetary stability, as here advocated, would not, therefore, restore economic instability. On the contrary: by removing the governmental sources of fiscal and monetary volatility that set off economic contractions, it would reduce the external shocks to which the economy is subject. A balanced-budget policy, combined with a rule for monetary stability, would result in more, not less, stability of the economy.

Notes

1   A recent re-statement of this perspective is in W. H. Hutt, *A Rehabilitation of Say's Law*, Ohio University Press, Athens, Ohio, 1974. 'Say's Equality' (after J. B. Say, the French 19th-century classical economist) is usually summarised as the proposition that 'supply creates its own demand', provided that markets operate in a competitive manner.

2   The 'paradox of thrift' is the Keynesian proposition that a reduction in thriftiness (an increase in private or governmental spending propensities) will boost the economy.

3   A specific discussion of these two economic cosmologies is in Axel Leijonhufvud, 'Effective Demand Failures', *Swedish Journal of Economics 75*, March 1973, pp. 31–3.

4   'I am sure that the power of vested interests is vastly exaggerated compared with the gradual encroachment of ideas. Not, indeed, immediately, but after a certain interval; for in the field of economic and political philosophy there are not many who are influenced by new theories after they are 25 or 30 years of age, so that the ideas which civil servants and politicians and even agitators apply to current events are not likely to be the newest. But, soon or late, it is ideas, not vested interests, which are dangerous for good or evil.'(J. M. Keynes, *The General Theory of Employment, Interest and Money*, Macmillan, 1936, pp. 383–4.)

5   A thorough survey of this shift in paradigm toward fiscal policy in the United States is in Herbert Stein, *The Fiscal Revolution in America*, University of Chicago Press, Chicago, 1969.

6   'We have seen that he [Keynes] was strongly imbued with what I have called the presuppositions of Harvey Road. One of these presuppositions may perhaps be summarised in the idea that the government of Britain was and would continue to be in the hands of an intellectual aristocracy using the method of persuasion.' (The late Sir Roy Harrod, *The Life of John Maynard Keynes*, Macmillan, 1951, pp. 192–3.) Harvey Road was the location of the Keynes family residence in Cambridge.

7   *Ibid.*, p. 193.

8   A fuller examination of the similarities and differences is in James M. Buchanan, 'Individual Choice in Voting and the Market', *Journal of Political Economy 62*, August 1954, pp. 334–43; reprinted in *idem, Fiscal Theory and Political Economy*, University of North Carolina Press, Chapel Hill, 1960, pp. 90–104.

9   This point about the categorical difference between present and future has been a theme of many of the writings of G. L. S. Shackle. A terse statement appears in his *Epistemics and Economics*, Cambridge University Press, 1972, p. 245: 'We cannot have experience of actuality at two distinct "moments". The moment of actuality, the moment in being, "the present", is *solitary*. Extended time, beyond "the moment", appears in this light as a figment, a product of thought' (Shackle's italics).

10 And even to the extent that citizens do creatively imagine such alternative, conjectural futures, democratic budgetary processes may produce a different form of bias against the surplus. To the extent that budgetary institutions permit fragmented appropriations, for instance, a 'prisoner's dilemma' (in which choices made by each person individually will produce undesirable results compared with what would result if all made a common choice) will tend to operate to dissipate revenues that might produce a budget surplus. Suppose, for instance, that a potential $10 billion budget surplus is prevented from arising due to the presentation of 10 separate spending proposals of $1 billion each, as opposed to the presentation of a single expenditure proposal of $10 billion. In the first case, although each participant may recognise that he would be better off if none of the spending proposals carry, institutions that allow separate, fragmented budgetary consideration may operate to create a result that is mutually undesirable, akin to the prisoner's dilemma. An analysis of this possibility is in James M. Buchanan and Gordon Tullock, *The Calculus of Consent*, University of Michigan Press, Ann Arbor, 1962, especially ch. 10.

11 Discussed for instance, by Daniel R. Vining and Thomas C. Elwertowski, 'The Relationship between Relative Prices and the General Price Level', *American Economic Review* 66, September 1976, pp. 699–708.

12 A popular, textbook abstraction of the nature of macro-economic policy originated by Professor Don Patinkin.

13 For example, Friedrich A. Hayek, *Monetary Theory and the Trade Cycle*, Harcourt Brace, New York, 1932; and *idem, Prices and Production*, 2nd edn, Routledge and Kegan Paul, 1935.

14 Much of this is discussed in Richard E. Wagner, 'Economic Manipulation for Political Profit: Macroeconomic Consequences and Constitutional Implications', *Kyklos* 30, 3, 1977, pp. 395–410.

15 Further discussion of the neglect of the real world of complex micro-relations in orthodox macro-economic analysis is in L. M. Lachmann, *Macro-economic Thinking and the Market Economy*, Hobart Paper 56, IEA, 1973.

16 See particularly such works by Henri Bergson as *Essai sur les données immédiates de la conscience*, F. Alcan, Paris, 1899; and *idem, L'Evolution créatrice*, F. Alcan, Paris, 1907. A related treatment within the context of economic analysis is in G. L. S. Shackle, *Decision, Order, and Time in Human Affairs*, Cambridge University Press, 1961.

17   *Prices and Production*, Routledge & Kegan Paul, 1931.

18   [Camelot was the capital of King Arthur's ideal society of chivalric literature from the 10th to the 13th centuries. It proved unfeasible because good intentions belied human nature. – Ed.]

19   This theme is stated in Frank H. Knight, *Intelligence and Democratic Action*, Harvard University Press, Cambridge, Mass., 1960, and G. Warren Nutter, *Where Are We Headed?*, Reprint No. 34, American Enterprise Institute, Washington DC, 1975, originally published in the *Wall Street Journal*, 10 January 1975.

20   J. Enoch Powell, 'Plan to Spend First; Find the Money Later', *Lloyds Bank Review*, April 1959.

21   *Democracy and the Value of Money: The Theory of Money from Locke to Keynes*, Occasional Paper 53, IEA, 1977.

22   A specific proposal along these lines is discussed by N. W. Duck and D. K. Sheppard, 'A Proposal for the Control of the UK Money Supply', *Economic Journal*, March 1978, pp. 1–17.

23   I. and F. L. Adelman, 'The Dynamic Properties of the Klein–Goldberger Model', *Econometrica*, October 1959; A. Goldberger, *Impact Multipliers and Dynamic Properties of the Klein–Goldberger Model*, North Holland, 1959; B. G. Hickman (ed.), *Econometric Models of Cyclical Behaviour*, National Bureau of Economic Research, 1971.

24   D. Williams, 'Montague Norman and Banking Policy in the Nineteen Twenties', *Yorkshire Bulletin of Economic and Social Research*, July 1959, p.46.

25   D. Winch, *Economics and Policy: A Historical Study*, Hodder and Stoughton, 1969, p. 75.

26   *A Monetary History of the United States, 1867–1960*, National Bureau of Economic Research, 1963, Ch. 7; this chapter has also been published separately as *The Great Contraction*, Princeton University Press, Princeton, NJ, 1965.

6

The Inconsistencies of the National Health Service: a Study in the Conflict between Individual Demand and Collective Supply

1 Introduction

To a detached observer in 1965, Great Britain's 17-year experiment in providing 'free' health services exhibits many signs of failure. In July 1965, an overwhelming majority of the delegates to the Swansea meeting of the British Medical Association supported a resolution calling for the introduction of privately-collected fees from patients, recoverable from the state, to be included as one method of remuneration in the 'doctors' charter' at present under negotiation with the Minister of Health. Even before this unpredicted and unexpected expression of professional opposition, the Association held the undated resignations of nearly 18,000 family doctors (out of a total of 23,000) pending the outcome of negotiations on many points with the Minister. Relatively fewer numbers are entering the medical profession each year, and the emigration of British-trained doctors continues.[1] The number of practising doctors declined by 300 from October 1963 to October 1964 in the face of a substantial net increase in population. Resident staff in British hospitals has come increasingly to be composed of immigrants, mostly from India and Pakistan. Hospital facilities are overcrowded, and long delays in securing treatment, save for strictly emergency cases, are universally noted.

What are the reasons for these apparent failures in the system for which so much was hoped in 1948? Why do the ideals of the late 1940s remain so far out of reach, even after 17 years? Some such understanding is essential if anything other than gimcrack reforms are to be introduced. Recent events in the United States and in Canada make it additionally

Published originally as IEA Occasional Paper No. 7 (1965).

important to evaluate and interpret British experience correctly. In 1965, also in July, the United States embarked upon its own programme of national government financing of medical care for the aged. The Canadian government is actively considering proposals to provide major federal aid to provincial health-service systems. Can similar failures be predicted in these two cases?

There are three possible explanations of the apparent failure of the National Health Service. Are the undesirable features observed in the British system due to mistakes in administering the health services, mistakes that 'wiser' men or parties could have avoided? Are these difficulties due to the very structure of the institutions through which health services are provided, and which could, therefore, be removed only after major reforms in this institutional structure? Or, finally, are these difficulties inherent in the nature of the health services themselves? Can services that are privately valued by individuals – 'personal' services – be provided 'free' by governments?

I shall argue that only the second of these questions needs to be answered affirmatively. The observed failures of the NHS can be explained by the *structure of the institutions*. This suggests that, at best, improvements in administration can provide only short-term palliatives. Explanations are not to be found in either wrong-headed decisions by ministers or short-sighted policies of political parties. Governments that remain broadly democratic can be successful in providing 'free' services, but only if they do so within institutions that promote general consistency in the social decision-making process. In models that approximate to the British structure, I shall explain the observed results by showing that in their *private or individual choice* behaviour as potential users or demanders of health-medical services, individuals are inconsistent with their *public or collective choice* behaviour as potential voters-taxpayers who make decisions on supplying these same services. The individuals who are the demanders and those who are the suppliers are, of course, basically the same persons acting in two separate rôles, and the facts themselves suggest the inconsistency. My central point is that this inconsistency does not in any way reflect irrationality on the part of individual decision-makers, but that it arises exclusively from the institutional setting for choice on the two sides of the account. Once this relatively simple point is recognised and accepted, the directions for possible constructive reforms become clear.

My discussion is limited to institutional theory. I shall not discuss either the historical development of the NHS or its descriptive characteristics at present. The discussion is also positive; I shall not be concerned here with the normative question as to how health services 'should' be organised, privately or publicly. In what follows, I shall first review briefly the traditional principle of neo-classical public finance that is relevant for the analysis of the NHS. The implications normally drawn from the application of this principle will be noted, emphasising the contrast between the inferred neo-classical predictions and the British experience. The reasons for the refutation of these predictions are shown to lie in economists' failure to analyse political choice-processes. The individual and the collective settings for individual choice behaviour are examined in some detail, and models that seem to typify the British example will be presented. Finally, brief attention will be given to alternative institutional arrangements that might eliminate the fundamental inconsistencies.

2 The Elasticity Principle

If the price elasticity of individual demand, i.e. the responsiveness to a (small) change in price, is significantly higher than zero over the applicable range, governments cannot efficiently 'give away' goods or services. This is one of the most widely accepted principles in the theory of public finance. It is found in most modern text books, but it also finds authority in such respected neo-classical writers as Pigou and Wicksell.[2] Within its traditional setting, the principle is valid. If government tries to supply goods or services that are privately divisible among separate persons at zero prices to users, the quantity demanded by all individuals in the aggregate will be significantly larger than the quantity that would be demanded at prices set by (marginal) cost, except where the price elasticity approaches zero.

For some goods and services, this required elasticity condition is satisfied. For example, the government could, without undue losses in efficiency, provide 'free' funeral services, for the very simple reason that each person dies only once; a zero price does not produce a larger demand for funerals than a high (or even a low) price. For other goods and services, 'free' provision would obviously be impossible, for example, beefsteaks, motor cars, and minks. Between such extremes as these, various goods and services may be arrayed in terms of predicted elasticity coefficients over the relevant ranges of prices. Education, for example, can within limits be made available free of direct user charges because each child can 'demand' only one year's quantity of service per year.[3]

Medical-health services clearly fall somewhere along the spectrum between education and motor cars. For certain types of medical care, price elasticity may be low indeed; there should be approximately the same number of broken legs treated under zero and under marginal-cost prices. For other types of health service, however, price elasticity may be relatively high. The British experience suggests that the demands for drugs[4] and for consultation by general practitioners and possibly for hospital care fall into this category. For medical-health services taken as an undifferentiated whole, individuals will be led to demand significantly larger quantities at zero user prices than they would demand at positive prices.[5] This part of the neo-classical principle amounts to nothing more than a straightforward application of the first law of demand.

But there is more to be said about the principle. It states that governments cannot *efficiently* give away goods and services that do not satisfy the required elasticity condition. In this form, the principle says nothing at all about the manner in which the inefficiencies will be generated when this condition is not met, or about the final incidence of such inefficiencies. Economists have normally assumed that these inefficiencies would take the form of relatively excessive investment in supplying the services in question. This assumption represents a simple extension of consumer-sovereignty models in which supply is expected always to adjust to demand over the long run. The presumption has been that, should governments try to give away services that fail to meet the required elasticity condition, they will find it necessary to extend supply to meet expressed demand, even at the expense of relative over-investment in the services. In responding to 'needs' criteria at zero user prices, governments would have been predicted to devote relatively too much public outlay to the provision of such divisible, personal services as medical care, 'too much' being measured against the standard criteria for allocating resource use of consumer preferences as expressed in the market. The alternative response that governments might make in such situations seems rarely to have been considered. They may make decisions on the supply of the service independently of the demands for the service, and on the basis of quite different considerations. As a result, the inefficiencies may take the form of deterioration in the *quality* of the services themselves, including congestion of available facilities.

3 External Economies

A second, and, to some extent, independent, principle has emerged from theoretical economics, and finds its origin in Pigou's discussion of external economies and diseconomies.[6] When an activity generates significant external economies, individual or private organisation has been held to generate relative under-investment. The standard Pigovian inference is that a lower-than-optimal amount of the activity will take place. Medical-health services have been classified by many economists as being such that private or individual organisation produces significant external economies. This is, of course, the argument that has been thought to provide the economic rationale for a shift from private organisation to public or collective organisation. Under the latter, presumably, the relevant external effects can be internalised in the collective-decision process. The orthodox Pigovian prediction would be that such a shift in organisation, from private to public, would result in substantial increases in outlay on providing the services.[7]

4 The Neo-classical Prediction

The two strands of economic analysis sketched above become mutually reinforcing when prediction is made concerning the direction of change in the total resources used in medical services that would result from substituting a socialised or nationalised service for a privately-organised service, in whole or in part. The welfare economist, concentrating his attention on the predicted presence of external economies and ignoring problems of collective decision-making, predicts that such a change in organisation will increase the resources invested from sub-optimal to optimal levels. The traditional public finance theorist might agree with the welfare economist, but, being somewhat more sophisticated as regards attention to political decisions, and recognising the elasticity conditions, he predicts that governments will tend to expand investment *beyond* optimal limits. In trying to meet expressed 'needs' for or demands on the available facilities, substantial over-investment might take place. The sophisticated neo-classical economist, taking both of these considerations into account, would have seemed on quite safe grounds in predicting that, after 1948, total outlay on health-medical services in

Great Britain would increase substantially *relative to that which would have been made under the alternatives.*

Experience in Great Britain so far does not corroborate such neo-classical predictions that might have been, and were, made.[8] Since 1948, total outlay on medical-health care has increased less in Great Britain than in the United States, where it is supplied largely in the market, even after all of the appropriate statistical adjustments for income-wealth levels, population, etc., are made.[9] The task before us becomes that of 'explaining' why these predictions failed. For this purpose, it is not necessary to discuss further the theory of external economies and its possible application to the organisation of medical-health services. Such discussion becomes relevant to the normative question concerning the efficient method of organising the services and to the comparative results of alternative structures. The aim here is much more limited; we seek only to understand the broad pattern of results that are observed under the British experiment of collectivising the health services, results that are at variance with the neo-classical predictions. We can do this by concentrating on elementary analysis.

The central part of the elasticity principle seems to be corroborated. At zero levels of user price, individuals are observed to demand relatively large quantities of health services, and we may presume that these quantities would be substantially reduced upon the establishment of positive charges. (Experience with drug fees alone suggests this result.) The neo-classical prediction relating to *individual* or *private* responses to the provision of 'free' health services does not therefore seem to be challenged by the evidence.

It is in relation to the *public* or *collective* responses to these demands that predictions seem to have gone astray. Responsible *collective*, i.e. governmental, decision-makers have not expanded investment in sup-plying health services to the levels of expressed *individual* demands. The inefficiencies that have arisen are clearly not in the form of excessive total outlay on the health services. The British experience strongly suggests that, rather than responding to 'needs' through increases in aggregate supply, governments have chosen to allow the quality of services to deteriorate rapidly, both in some appropriate, physically measurable sense[10] and in terms of congestion costs imposed on pro-spective consumers.

The failures of the National Health Service are not exhibited by a disproportionately large fraction of British resources being drained away through investment in supplying it; the failures are exhibited by breakdowns in the quality of the services themselves due to the disparity between the facilities supplied and the demands made upon them.

5 Democratic Choice Process

Could this combination of results have been predicted by a more satisfactory model of choice behaviour? Can the observed pattern of results be explained? I shall show that explanation becomes possible when a plausible model for democratic choice process is added. We must extend the standard theory so that we can say something about the predicted responses of individuals in their capacities as participants in *collective* or group decisions. Only when this step is taken can we make some elementary predictions about the reactions of governments to privately expressed demands on health facilities and services.

The evidence suggests that the neo-classical inference that governments respond straightforwardly to 'needs' is invalid. Economists have not examined either this inference or that of theoretical welfare economics (that governments act 'optimally') carefully because analysis of the political-choice mechanism has been held to be outside their range of competence. Institutional and policy analysis in both neo-classical and Keynesian economics has suffered because of this implicit refusal to extend the model of individual choice behaviour. The result has been a sharp distinction between the choice behaviour of the individual in market processes and his behaviour in political processes. Implicitly, analysis has presumed that governmental decisions are divorced from the preferences of individual citizens. The first requirement for a more sophisticated explanation of observed experience is an explicit construction of a model for the political-decision process.

In any system that is properly described by the much-abused word 'democratic', political decision must ultimately be made by the individuals who hold membership in the politically or collectively organised group. Individuals make choices in two separate capacities, as buyers–sellers in ordinary markets for *private* goods and services, and as buyers–sellers of *public* goods and services in the political process. Only within recent years has rigorous analysis come to be applied to the second type of individual choice behaviour.[11] An economic theory of collective decision-making remains in its infancy, but, even with the rudimentary models that are available, significant advances in an understanding of the general results of democratic political systems can be made.

At any general level, analysis of political process must take some account of the rules and the institutions through which separate individual choices, whether directly or indirectly expressed, are combined so as to produce results that, once selected, are uniformly imposed on all members of the political unit. Obviously, different rules can produce decisively different results, even should the underlying structure of individual preferences remain unchanged. Economy in explanation at the very beginning of analysis, however, may be gained by neglecting the necessarily complex examination of alternative rules. Such an examination should not be introduced until the explanatory potential of simpler models has been exhausted. In certain cases it may be possible to explain phenomena of the real world satisfactorily through reliance on single-person models, that is, through an analysis limited to the choice behaviour of a single, isolated individual as he participates in political process. If such an analysis works there is no need to resort to more complicated interactions under collective-decision rules, despite the possible emergence of additional explanatory potential.

I hope to show that the observed experience of the NHS can be satisfactorily explained by analysing the behaviour of the individual citizen, as a demander of health services on the one hand and as a potential voter on the other. Considerations of the way in which his preferences are translated into government policy in the political process are not needed. In other words, the results are those that would emerge from the rational calculus of the individual as private or individual demander and as public or collective supplier of health services. For clarity, the model to be discussed could be assumed one in which all individuals are identical to the single person, or, alternatively, one in which the single person is genuinely 'representative' of the whole community.

Consider now a single individual. He participates in both market decisions and political decisions. In the former he chooses the quantities of private goods and services he will buy or sell, demand or supply. He will do so individualistically and privately, and the divisibility of the goods and services ensures that he can act separately and independently from other persons. The individual can select his own most preferred level of consumption of, say, beer, without in any way deciding or even affecting what any one, or all, of his fellow citizens shall consume. In the second capacity, as a participant in the political process, the individual also chooses the quantities of public goods and services that he will demand and supply. But here he will do so as a member of a group. Although his own preferences will determine the manner of his voting, the outcomes must be applied to *all* members of the group. A choice implies, therefore, a willingness to finance stated quantities of a good or service for all members of the group through appropriately chosen taxes also levied on all members.

Nothing more than a cursory examination of the institutions of the NHS is required to recognise that an individual is placed in the position of demanding medical-health services in a market-like choosing capacity. The 'market' he confronts presents him with opportunities of selecting preferred quantities of services at zero prices. He chooses individualistically and privately, and, on the *demand* side, 'free' health services are treated in much the same way as 'free' beer, that is, the demand would swell more or less rapidly. At the same time, however, the individual as a participant in collective-political choice, as a voter–taxpayer–beneficiary, must indicate his decision on the aggregate quantity of medical-health services to be supplied to the community as a whole. In this capacity he cannot select an outcome for himself that will not also be applicable for everyone else. On the *supply* side, medical-health services are not 'free' in any sense of the word; on the contrary, they are severely limited by consideration of all the other alternatives – more schools, better housing, larger pensions – that would have to be sacrificed if they were expanded solely in response to demand at zero prices.

Once this essential splitting of the individual's decision is recognised, the inconsistency in results is not at all strange. Indeed, this inconsistency is precisely what careful analysis would lead us to predict.

6 The Individual as Private Demander and Public Supplier

Why will the individual demand more services privately than he will supply publicly? This is the kernel of the internal conflict in the National Health Service.

We may first concentrate on his behaviour in demanding services made available to him by the community at zero user prices. What will determine the quantity demanded? One of the first lessons in elementary economics provides the answer. The rational person will extend his demands on such services to the point at which the marginal utility becomes zero: that is, so long as additional services promise to yield positive benefits, there will be no incentive for the individual to restrict his 'purchases'. But, one may say, this sort of behaviour will be 'malingering', the word commonly heard in 1965 British comments on the health service. Should not the individual consumer, or prospective consumer, recognise that, when he extends his own private demands to such limits, he uses up resources that are valuable to the community and for which the community must pay?

The individual who is well informed may well recognise that his own behaviour in this respect will commit valuable resources.[12] This point is not in question, and our explanation does not depend on ignorance to explain the observed results. Accurate recognition and measurement of the social costs of health-medical services will in no way modify the behaviour of the individual in demanding such services. Faced with no direct user charges, he will not find it personally advantageous to restrict his own demands, although he may fully appreciate that the value of these services to him is less than the cost imposed on the whole community in supplying them. The individual's behaviour in this case is precisely equivalent to that of the person who refuses to contribute voluntarily to the financing of a mutually desired purely public or purely collective good (the 'free-rider' who benefits whether he pays or not).[13]

In either of these two situations, the individual, indeed each and every individual, may recognise full well that he, along with *all* of his fellows, would be better off if *everyone*, in practice, behaved differently. But there is nothing he is able to do, individually and voluntarily, to affect the way in which others behave.[14] If he decides, privately and personally, to reduce his own demands on the services, for reasons of 'social conscience', he will be acting irrationally. But since his behaviour will not, in itself, modify the behaviour of others in the aggregate, he will be forgoing opportunities for personal gains, however slight, without benefiting others to any measurable extent. Under choice conditions such as these, it is not at all surprising that what is called 'malingering' is widely observed.

Let us now shift our attention to the behaviour of the same individual, who is assumed to be both informed and rational, as he participates directly or indirectly in the political-choice process. We may consider his participation in decisions on the supply of health services independently from his participation in decisions on other issues for collective action. He must indicate his preferences, in some voting or quasi-voting process, among alternative health-service budgets, each of which embodies a specific quantity of services to be made available for the whole community, and each of which, in turn, embodies an implied levy of taxes sufficient to finance the matching quantity. How much taxation will the individual prefer in combination with how much total outlay on the health services?

To the extent that he is well-informed, the individual can make some reasonably accurate translation between the tax or cost side and the level of health-service benefits that may be provided. He will know, roughly, what level of tax rates will be required to finance each level of health-service budget and, in turn, what quantity of aggregate services each budget will supply. But what will determine his own choice among budgets? The individual's own preferences will be controlling here as they are in private choice, but here he cannot choose between positions for himself independently from or in isolation from the positions of all others in the political group. Here choice involves indicating a preference for one *group* outcome over the others, even though this choice may be largely determined by the individual's own position in this outcome. Each alternative for choice embodies results not only for the participating or 'voting' individual but also for all others. Each budget defines a specific expected level of services along with a specific expected level of taxation, along with a distribution in both cases.

This is a choice setting that is categorically different from that which characterises the demand side. In his capacity as a participant in collective choice, the individual must *balance costs against benefits*. He will try, as best he can, to estimate the tax costs that various levels of service will impose on him and he will weigh these against estimates of benefits that he will secure from these various levels. Clearly any choice on the individual's part here to extend supply to the point where the marginal utility from the services becomes zero would be foolish because the sacrifice of alternatives would be relatively enormous. The individual will quite rationally indicate a preference for an aggregate supply of services that falls below such satiation levels. His choice, in a political-decision context, will be for a quantity of gross investment in health services much lower than that which would be required by a policy of providing constant-quality services to the extent indicated by privately expressed 'needs'.[15]

7 Application to British Experience

I suggest that the observed breakdown in the NHS can at least be partially explained by the theory of institutional choice outlined above. The politicians who have made the decisions on investment in the health services have been simply responding to the preferences of individual citizens. The observed results are precisely those that the theory would have enabled us to predict. Alternative hypotheses concerning the behaviour of politicians can, of course, be advanced, and some of them might be of explanatory value. My emphasis is on the point that no supplemental hypotheses are required; the experience can be explained by postulating that politicians behave 'as if' they transmit the preferences of citizens into political outcomes.

As indicated at several places, the first half of the theory is a straight-forward application of one of the most elementary of economic principles, about which there will surely be little or no debate. The novelty or innovation in this analysis lies in its extension of what is essentially economic reasoning to political decisions. This economic theory of politics remains unfamiliar territory, but we are fortunate here in that no complex models seem to be needed to explain satisfactorily the health-service experience. There has been no need to resort to models of majority rule, of parliamentary systems of government, of political parties, of political leadership. This is not to deny that some such models might provide equally satisfactory explanations of real-world results. One of the fundamental methodological principles for all science, however, is that of accepting the simplest possible hypothesis when a genuine choice among explanations is possible. All that has been necessary here is a simple acknowledgement that individual preferences are influential in determining political outcomes. The results suggest that the transmission of these preferences into outcomes does take place, quite independently of the particular way in which this process operates.

This is merely another way of stating that the British political order is assumed to be effectively 'democratic'. The theory cannot be used simultaneously to explain the results from a democratic political model and to prove that the system is, in fact, democratic. If a *dirigiste*, non-democratic political structure is postulated, explanation of the observed results would necessarily be different.

8 Directions for Reform

If the explanation advanced in this *Paper* is accepted, the directions for reform in the institutions of the NHS are indicated. The inconsistency between demand-choice and supply-choice must be eliminated, and the individual, as the ultimate chooser, must be placed in positions where the two parts of what is really a single decision are not arbitrarily separated. This can be accomplished only if an explicit decision on demand is allowed to call forth or to imply specific supply response, or if an explicit decision on supply embodies a specific demand response. The splitting into two parts of what must be, in the final analysis, a single decision must be removed.

To illustrate that any arbitrary splitting of the demand–supply decision will create inconsistency, we may examine the various alternatives other than the one found in practice. Suppose, as our first example, that an attempt should be made to provide health services 'free', as currently, but that, also, an attempt should be made to cover the costs of these services through 'free' contributions, without the imposition of coercive taxes. In this situation, individuals would have health services freely made available to them but they would also be allowed freely to make whatever contributions they choose toward financing them. Predicted results of this institutional combination are obvious. Relatively little would be collected in contributions, since all individuals would be placed in 'free-rider' positions. The system would be characterised by gross under-supply and gross over-demand, with resulting deterioration in quality in all respects. The institutional combination in being embodies only one-half of this worst possible system.

As a second illustrative example of a split-decision structure, let us suppose that, as in the preceding case, individuals are asked to make voluntary contributions but that, on the demand side, decisions are made publicly, not privately. The government would, in this situation, place restrictive limits on the use of the health services, but there would be no collective decision on the total amount to be supplied. This structure need not exhibit quality deterioration due to excessive individual demand, but the aggregate quantity of health services would be grossly inadequate and much below that quantity which would satisfy criteria for the optimal use of resources. This institutional combination is mentioned here only because it represents the exact reverse of that which is in being; here there would be public or collective demand decisions and private or individual supply decisions. The inefficiencies would take a dramatically different form from those currently observed.

Any reasonably workable set of institutions must bring demand decisions and supply decisions into the same framework for individual choice. There are only two alternatives here. The first is to allow individuals to make both demand decisions and supply decisions privately. This amounts to treating medical-health services as private and allowing the ordinary institutions of the market to operate. Individuals would be allowed, as they now are, to adjust demands privately and independently, but not at zero prices. Instead, prices would be set by competitive forces and the services finally made available would be determined not through a collective-political decision but by the private decisions of many suppliers responding to expressed demands. This structure would be an efficient one in the restricted sense that no apparent shortages or surpluses would be observed.

Market organisation may not, however, take adequate account of the external economies in certain types of medical-health services. In addition, the distributive results of market organisation may not prove broadly acceptable and direct transfers of income-wealth to mitigate them may not be feasible. For either or both these reasons, or others, the market organisation of health services based on the distribution of income that emerges from a market economy may be rejected.

The alternative institutional structure is one in which both the demand side and the supply side are joined in a collective or public choice process. If the market solution is rejected, this becomes the only avenue of reform. The institutions through which individuals are allowed to adjust demands privately and individually to zero-price health services must be eliminated, and a specific collective decision on aggregate supply or quantity of services must be made to embody a specific quality of final services distributed in a specific manner among individuals. This means that the government must decide, collectively, how much health services each member of the group shall have available to him. There must be some determinate allocation of final services among persons, either in physical quantity units or in more flexible units of general purchasing power. In the first case, each individual would be allowed to utilise specific maximum quantities per year: x visits to the surgery; y minor operations; z days in hospital. In the second case, each individual would be allowed to utilise a total 'value' of service of P pounds per year as he chooses among the various health services. This scheme would allow for a somewhat wider individual range of choice among health-service facilities, but it would require, of course, the assigning of specific 'shadow prices' to the different services made available. Either of these two schemes would, however, eliminate the institutional inefficiencies that are currently observed. There need be no congestion of available facilities and no continuing deterioration in service standards. The allowable demand on the facilities would be limited by the supply decision, and that would be that.

The objections to these modifications in existing institutions stem from the failure to allow for individuals who may desire, privately or personally, to utilise more health-medical services than any collective or political determination of allowable limits would provide. Such a desire, or need, may be due to fortuitous circumstances, and it may be largely independent of user price in many instances. If a collective limit of 30 days in hospital is imposed, what about the person whose illness requires 60 days?

Considerable improvements may be made in overcoming such objections if the many separate categories of health services are differentiated and treated separately. In general terms, however, this genuine problem of above-limit demands under any publicly-financed system of health services can only be met by allowing for a market or market-like set of institutions to emerge which supplements the publicly financed, publicly supplied facilities. The advantages of such a system are that there need be no limits placed on the total amount of health services to be utilised by any single person or family; the necessity for limits applies only to the total amount of health services that shall be *publicly* financed and/or *publicly* supplied for him. Over and beyond these limits, the individual may be allowed to choose as much or as little as he desires, and for any reason.

Any detailed discussion of the particular features of the combined institutional structure that seems indicated as relatively efficient would require a second paper. One implication of the argument may be noted. Consideration should be given to an institutional structure that replaces, in whole or in part, direct public or governmental supply and operation by *public financing* of privately-organised operation. This structure would allow for greater flexibility in individual adjustments while, at the same time, it would facilitate bringing the demand side and the supply side more closely into co-ordination, in both public and private choices. On the basis of externality, equity, or other arguments, a political or collective decision can be made on the aggregate quantity of health services that will be *publicly financed*, and this decision can include a set of maximum limits, defined in purchasing power units, that will be made available to each person. These need not, of course, be equal among separate persons and groups. Individuals could be provided with vouchers for these indicated limits, which they could then utilise in purchasing health services as they chose. To the extent that their demands exceeded the amounts that could be purchased for such limits, individuals would be able to extend utilisation by privately financed supplements, these being financed directly by paying fees or charges or through various possible private insurance schemes.

My concern is not with recommending the institutional structure that

Great Britain 'should' adopt. The various institutional reforms above are mentioned to illustrate that an efficient NHS *can be organised* once the inconsistencies are recognised. Under a continuation of the existing structure the observed inefficiencies are likely to become more and more serious over time.

Appendix: Criteria for Aggregate Investment in Health Services

There are two distinct elements of the British experience that seem to refute the normative implications of neo-classical welfare economics. These are the failures of total investment in health services to rise demonstrably above that which would have been forthcoming under private organisation, and the willingness of governments to allow apparent quality deterioration including increasing congestion of available facilities. This *Paper* has been limited to an explanation of the second of these elements.

In a paper published in 1963, written jointly with Milton Kafoglis of the University of Florida, an hypothesis was advanced that can partially 'explain' the first of these two characteristic elements of the British experience. National Health Service data were cited as illustrative of the more general argument. It may be helpful here to summarise the argument of the Buchanan–Kafoglis paper and to relate it to that which this *Paper* advances.

The Buchanan–Kafoglis analysis was concerned with comparing total outlay on a service under private and under public organisation when, at the margin of private extension, there are significant external economies. Whether or not such external economies characterise medical care in general need not be discussed in detail here. Some types of service, notably prevention of communicable diseases, seem clearly to exhibit such external economies, and, if necessary, the argument can be restricted in application to them. The orthodox Pigovian and post-Pigovian theorems about the divergence between marginal private and marginal social products suggest that an organisational shift from the private sector to the public sector would result in an increase in total resource commitment to the service in question. Implicitly, the whole analysis assumes that collective decision-makers would invest 'optimally'. The Buchanan–Kafoglis argument did not modify this implied assumption about collective decision-making. The argument showed, however, that a distinction between resource inputs and consumption output is required. The presence of significant external economies implies that outputs should be increased but, if 'efficiencies' in utilising inputs are produced by a shift from private to public organisation, total resource commitment may not be increased by this shift from a sub-optimal to an optimal position.

The argument was illustrated by a medical-care example. Consider the case of a highly communicable disease the spread of which can be prevented only by improved sanitation measures. In this situation, the community may find that collectivisation of the service, with the component change in *distribution* of total resource investment, provides for a greater than one-for-one substitute for individuals' previously undertaken outlays. The superior efficiencies may be such that the optimally distributed investment generates optimal outputs with less resources than private investment. This result need not, of course, be present, but the analysis suggests that organisational–institutional changes that effectively internalise external economies need not imply expanded overall resource commitment.

What does this analysis signify for the experience of the NHS? It suggests that the relatively limited total outlay on the provision of medical-health facilities since 1948 does not, in itself, imply that the aggregate investment is sub-optimal. To the extent that external economies characterised the pre-1948 organisation of the services, the change in distributional efficiency achieved under general collectivisation may have been sufficient to guarantee optimal supplies at observed levels of outlay. On the other hand, to the extent that relevant external economies did not characterise pre-1948 experience, no such increased distributional efficiency should have taken place. But, in this case, there is no economic argument, as such, for collectivisation and the private or market organisation tends to generate optimal levels of supply. The analysis suggests, therefore, that, regardless of the extent to which relevant external economies might have been present under private organisation, no implication can be drawn concerning relative levels of outlay required for 'optimality'.

If comparative levels of overall investment in medical-health care since 1948 tell us nothing at all about the attainment of the socially desired or optimal provision, how can the 'wisdom' of collective decision-makers after 1948 be evaluated? Here we resort to the second element that is observed, namely, congestion on the available facilities. Does this congestion, in itself, tell us anything? Does it suggest that total investment is sub-optimal? No such inference is possible. The congestion that is observed indicates only that the supply of medical-health services at a standard quality is not sufficient to meet demand at zero user prices. But, since zero user prices are not demonstrably optimal in themselves, there is no implication that the supply of standard-quality services sufficient to meet all demands at these prices would produce optimal levels of investment.

Therefore, if we look at the experience of the NHS in the framework of theoretical welfare economics, we can infer nothing at all concerning the 'correctness' or 'incorrectness' of the collective decisions that have been made as regards overall or aggregate levels of provision. The observed facts are consistent with either non-optimal or optimal levels of investment since 1948.

The distribution of the services made available must be sharply distinguished from the aggregate levels of supply. It seems highly unlikely, of course, that this distribution has been 'efficient' or 'optimal' since, as the analysis of the present *Paper* shows, the results depend on the private adjustments of many separate persons. The collectivisation of demand decisions might or might not involve a larger resource commitment; it would almost certainly involve a modified pattern of distributing the services that are made available.

Applied to the economics of health services, the emphasis of the earlier Buchanan–Kafoglis paper was on the question: What do the observed facts tell us about the level of total resource usage as measured in terms of the standard criteria of theoretical welfare economics? The answer is: Nothing at all.

The emphasis of the present *Paper* has been quite different and is on the question: Can the observed facts be explained satisfactorily in terms of simple models of private and public choice?

The dominant weakness of the NHS is not the inefficiencies of public or collective decisions. It is rather the inconsistency between these decisions and the private or individual decisions on the demand side.

Notes

1   See J. R. Seale, 'Medical Emigration: A Study in the Inadequacy of Official Statistics', in *Lessons from Central Forecasting*, Eaton Paper 6, IEA, October 1965.

2   A. C. Pigou, *A Study in Public Finance*, Macmillan, 1928; Knut Wicksell, *Finanztheoretische Untersuchungen*, Fischer, Jena, 1896.

3 For such services as funerals and education, individual demands for improvements in *quality* under zero user-pricing replace, to some extent, the more direct individual adjustments in *quantity* that are possible with goods and services falling along the opposite end of the array suggested. At best, however, these demands for quality improvements become pressures upon governments for change; they cannot, in themselves, consume resources.

4 Since the 2s. charge for prescriptions dispensed under the NHS was abolished on 1 February 1965, Ministry of Health figures show that prescriptions have risen 20 per cent in number and 28 per cent in cost compared with the same period of 1964; by comparison, certified sickness rose by only 7 per cent. The prescription charge was reintroduced in 1968 and was raised to £3.05 in April 1990.

5 [This is the economic theory behind the vague allusions by some sociologists to a 'price-barrier'. – Ed.]

6 A. C. Pigou, *The Economics of Welfare*, third edition, Macmillan, 1929.

7 In a paper previously published, Milton Kafoglis and I examined this hypothesis within the standard model of post-Pigovian welfare economics. We showed that total investment in supplying a service may not be increased by a shift from private to public organisation, even when the presence of relevant external economies is acknowledged. Our discussion centred on the necessity to distinguish inputs and outputs. We demonstrated that under certain assumptions about the substitutability between private and public provision in individuals' utility functions, overall efficiency might be increased without expansion in investment, even on the presumption that government decisions are fully correct. See James M. Buchanan and Milton Z. Kafoglis, 'A Note on Public Goods Supply', *American Economic Review*, June 1963, pp. 403–14. The argument developed in this earlier paper and its relationship to the discussion in the present *Paper* is summarised in the Appendix, pp. 128–30.

8 For example, Seymour Harris, 'The British Health Experiment: The First Two Years of the National Health Service', *American Economic Review*, May 1951, pp. 652–66.

9 See John and Sylvia Jewkes, *The Genesis of the British National Health Service*, Blackwell, 1961.

10 Physical measurement of quality is, of course, difficult in any setting, and notably so when research advances are as rapid as in medical care. Nevertheless it seems clear that quality of service, for example in British hospitals, has been allowed to deteriorate relative to that which would have been predicted to be present under a nationalised scheme.

11 For a list of some of the relevant works here, see the Suggestions for Further Reading on page 23 of *The Inconsistencies of the National Health Service*, particularly Section I.

12 Survey data indicate that individuals tend to be grossly uninformed about

the costs of publicly supplied medical services in Great Britain, and that there is a consistent tendency to underestimate these costs. This direction of error tends to accentuate the behavioural inconsistency discussed in this *Paper*. By contrast, there seems to be a consistent tendency for individuals to overestimate the costs of publicly-supplied education. See *Choice in Welfare*, IEA, 1963. *Choice in Welfare, 1965*, also indicates the degrees of knowledge or ignorance of the taxes paid and social benefits received by households of varying income and size.

13   In the modern theory of public finance, the individual behaviour in this situation is discussed at length as the 'free-rider problem'. See the references to this discussion in the Suggestions for Further Reading, Section II, p. 23 of *The Inconsistencies of the National Health Service*.

14   He finds himself caught in an *n*-person analogue to the familiar prisoners' dilemma, much discussed in modern game theory. See R. Duncan Luce and Howard Raiffa, *Games and Decisions*, Wiley, New York, 1958, pp. 94–102.

15   In this second choice situation, the individual is not in the *n*-person analogue to the prisoners' dilemma at all. Here the analogue would be the individual prisoner's voting choice for a standard 'policy for confessing' to be applied for all prisoners. The difference in the two choice situations for the individual creates inconsistency in results. There is no need for us to extend the analysis beyond the level of the single individual. We need not call upon the more complex models of group-choice for explanation.

Index